Teach Your Tot to Sign

Teach Your Tot to Sign

The Parents' Guide to American Sign Language

Stacy A. Thompson

Illustrations by Valerie Nelson-Metlay

Gallaudet University Press
Washington, D. C.

Gallaudet University Press
Washington, DC 20002

http://gupress.gallaudet.edu

Printed in Canada

Library of Congress Cataloging-in-Publication Data

Thompson, Stacy A.
Teach your tot to sign: the parents' guide to American Sign Language/Stacy A. Thompson;
illustrations by Valerie Nelson-Metlay.
p. cm.
Includes index.
ISBN 1-56368-311-3 (alk. paper)
1. American Sign Language – Study and teaching (Earl childhood) 2. American Sign Language – Vocabulary. 3. Nonverbal communication in children. 4. Infants – Language. 5. Toddlers – Language 6. Parent and child. I Nelson-Metlay, Val. II Title.
HV2474T492005
4197071–dc22

2004060848

∞ The paper used in this publication meets the minimum requirements of American National Standard for Information Sciences—Permanence of Paper for Printed Library Materials, ANSI Z39.48-1984.

This book is dedicated to the parents and teachers who are giving young children the gift of communication through American Sign Language.

Contents

Acknowledgments

I feel so blessed to have had the chance to write this book. There are many people who have helped me with the completion of this book. My heartfelt thanks go out to:

Val Nelson-Metlay for being so flexible with all of my additions to the word list. We started out with a little over 300 signs and ended up with over 500 signs. Thank you, Val, for your patience and all of your hard work on this book. You are a very talented artist.

Gallaudet University Press for accepting my idea and for publishing this book.

Ivey Pittle Wallace for being patient and for taking the time to answer all of my questions.

Kim Votry for helping me to get my foot in the door.

Joseph Garcia for starting a wonderful program that enables parents to sign with their babies.

Tom Thompson for being such a loving and devoted husband and father. You truly are amazing and I am so blessed to have married you. Thank you for being both the mommy and the daddy while I was working on this book.

Tyler, Catharine, and Daniel for making Mommy laugh every day and for loving me the way you do. You are my inspirations for this book. I love you all.

My family and friends for continuing to love, support, and pray for me even when I didn't ask. Thank you, Kyndal Lynn, for your smiles and for letting me borrow your pencil to write my book. Thank you, Braxton, for your thoughtfulness and for your humor.

My parents for your unconditional love and support. I love you.

My Savior, Jesus Christ. Thank you for your guidance and unconditional love. You always know what is best for me. None of this would have happened without you. I am truly blessed.

Stacy Thompson

Thank you for your support and patience: **Don, Danica, Monte, Boswell, Jaguar, and friends.**

Val Nelson-Metlay

Introduction

For several years, I have been teaching American Sign Language (also called ASL) classes to parents of hearing infants, parents of special needs children, and preschool teachers. During this time, many people have asked me if I knew of a book that had signs that were easy to make, a book that they could use with their young children at home and in the classroom. I searched in bookstores and on the Internet and found plenty of sign books, but none of them contained vocabulary that was geared toward children. To fill this void, I have created *Teach Your Tot to Sign,* a pocket-size book that includes signs for over 500 basic vocabulary words, such as *dinosaur, wagon,* and *pacifier.* It is easily portable and provides a resource parents can take with them anywhere.

This book will enable adults to communicate with young children, regardless of a child's hearing ability. Many children can benefit from using American Sign Language, including (but not limited to) deaf children, children with special needs or speech delays, and children who are learning English as a second language. Hearing infants and toddlers can benefit as well—they can begin to communicate with their parents by using signs before they are even able to speak. Imagine how thrilled you would be if your toddler could sign to you when she wants milk, or a book, or a diaper change. It is my hope that this book will help to open the pathway of communication between young children and the adults who care for them.

Learning to Sign

Before you begin to learn the signs in this book, there are a few things you should know about American Sign Language and signing. American Sign Language, or ASL, is the language used by deaf people in the United States. Each sign represents a specific concept or idea, just as each English word represents a specific concept or idea. However, some English words have more than one meaning. For example, the word *right* can mean a direction, an entitlement or privilege, or "correct." Since signs represent concepts, not English words, ASL has a different sign for each of these definitions. In this book, the meaning of the concept appears in parentheses next to the English word. For example, the entry for *right,* meaning a direction, looks like this: right (direction). The cross-referenced index at the back of the book will help you find the different signs to use with these English words.

Similarly, one sign can be used to represent several different English words. For example, the same sign is used for *bike, bicycle,* and *pedal.* When one sign is used to convey multiple English words, the words appear next to each other; so, for example, *bike, bicycle,* and *pedal* are listed together as one entry.

New signers often have questions about sign language and deaf people. Here's an informal list of some of those questions and their answers.

Frequently Asked Questions

Why should I use ASL with my hearing baby or toddler?

Signing with hearing babies and toddlers has become very popular in the past few years. It has been proven that babies as young as 6–7 months are able to communicate through sign language. Even though very young children have the ability to understand what their parents are saying to them, they have no way of expressing what they want, and this can cause a lot of frustration for them and their parents. Signing can reduce the frustration for the child as well as for the parents. Studies also have shown that signing with babies can accelerate their language development, create stronger bonds between the child and the parent, and build a child's self-esteem.

Where did American Sign Language come from?

American Sign Language is the native language of deaf people in the United States and parts of Canada. It is a beautiful and expressive language that developed from the interaction of deaf people at the American School for the Deaf in Hartford, Connecticut, which was the first school for deaf children in America. The first deaf teacher was Laurent Clerc, who came to the United States from France, where he had been a teacher at the school for deaf children in Paris. Clerc taught his French signs to the students at the American School, and they taught him the signs they used at home with their families and friends.

Why should I use ASL instead of making up my own signs?

There are a number of reasons why it is beneficial to utilize ASL rather than using made-up signs. First of all,

American Sign Language is already established. There is no need to make up signs when there are signs already available to you. One of the downfalls of using made-up signs is that it could be hard to remember which sign you used for a particular word. You will not have a resource to help you to remember the sign. With ASL, you have a variety of resources available to help you remember a specific sign.

Secondly, if a preschool teacher or playgroup leader teaches her students ASL signs, the child who knows made-up signs will be confused and frustrated when he doesn't understand the teacher and the other children. Another reason to use American Sign Language would be that you and your child can communicate with deaf and hard of hearing people. There are many deaf children mainstreamed into public schools. If children are taught ASL, they will be able to communicate with deaf and hard of hearing children in their schools. Deaf people are impressed when a hearing person tries to use their language. They will embrace and enjoy the fact that you are trying to use American Sign Language.

Are all signs the same across the United States?

Actually, most signs are the same but, like spoken languages, there are variations. For example, some people say *hoagies,* some say *subs,* and some say *grinders,* but they all mean the same thing. I live on the West Coast and use a W hand to sign *whale.* Val, the illustrator, lives on the East Coast and uses a Y hand to sign *whale.* If you have learned a sign and feel comfortable with it, use the sign that you know; other signers will understand you.

Can I use ASL anywhere in the world?

No, American Sign Language primarily is used in the United States and parts of Canada. Each country in the world has its own sign language. For example, China uses Chinese Sign Language, Mexico uses Mexican Sign Language, England uses British Sign Language, and so on. Some signs may be similar to American Sign Language, but most are different.

What is fingerspelling?

Deaf people often use their fingers to spell proper names and words that don't have signs. This is called *fingerspelling* because you spell a word letter by letter with your fingers. Each letter of the alphabet has a specific sign, and all the signs together make up the American Manual Alphabet (see page 10). Numbers also have specific signs, so you can count and do math problems with your fingers (see page 12). A great way to practice fingerspelling is to face the mirror and spell different words. You can also practice while riding in the car by spelling street names or store names.

Young children can benefit greatly from fingerspelling. It adds another dimension to their learning. Not only do they hear the word and see it in the air and on paper, but they feel the shapes of the letters they are making. All this enhances their learning ability.

Which hand should I use?

We all use one hand more than the other in carrying out our daily activities. This hand is called the dominant hand. In signing, the dominant hand makes all of the movements for one-hand signs and most of the movements for two-hand signs. The other hand acts as a base and is often stationary; it is called the passive hand. The signer in this book is right-handed, so all of the sign descriptions are written for a dominant right hand. If you are left-handed, reverse the directions to use your left hand as your dominant hand.

Why is it important to use facial expressions when I sign?

Facial expression is very important in American Sign Language. The face helps convey the true meaning of a sign. For example, when you sign *hot* to warn your child about a hot surface, you should have a stern expression on your face. When you sign *sad,* your face should show the emotion you are feeling.

You can also use your face to indicate the difference between making a statement and asking a question. When you ask a question that requires a yes or no answer, you raise your eyebrows. When you ask a Who, What, Where, How, When, or Why question, you squint your eyebrows and draw them together.

How to Use This Book

The signs are presented in English word order from A–Z. Each sign illustration is accompanied by the English translations of that sign as well as a description of how to make the sign. Additionally, many of the sign descriptions contain a memory aid and a tip. The index located at the back of the book contains all of the English synonyms connected with the signs in the book.

The sign descriptions are short and easy to understand. They are a verbal map of the illustration. The description and illustration go hand in hand. They work together to give you a complete picture of the sign. The memory aids will help you remember the signs. The tips are helpful hints ranging from reminders to alternate signs. Some signs have more than one tip, but not all signs have a tip and a memory aid.

Deciphering the Signs

Many signs begin with the hand (or hands) in one position or shape and end in a different position or shape. The shapes of the hands, or *handshapes,* come from the letters of the American Manual Alphabet and the manual numbers (see pages 10–12). There are also special handshapes, which are modifications of the letters and numbers (see page 11).

The sign descriptions will tell you which handshape to use for every sign. To help you see which position or handshape comes first, the illustrations in this book are drawn with broken lines and solid lines. The broken lines show the first position of the sign, and the solid lines indicate the final position. Sometimes the initial and final positions are very different, so you will see two drawings for these signs. The drawing on the left shows the first position and the drawing on the right shows the final position, as in the sign for *balloon.*

Many of the illustrations include arrows that show how and where the hands move. If the sign requires one movement, there is one arrow; if the movement repeats, there are two arrows (for example, the sign *more*). Once in a while, the hands outline a specific shape (like in *house*), and arrows for these signs are drawn with a broken line. Take care in following the direction of the arrows. If you move your hands in another direction, you could be making a completely different sign.

Ready, Set, Go

So, now you are ready to teach your tot to sign. Take the book with you wherever you go—to the store, the library, the playground, and day care. It's easy to use and fits nicely in the diaper bag! And best of all, it will enhance the bond between you and your child.

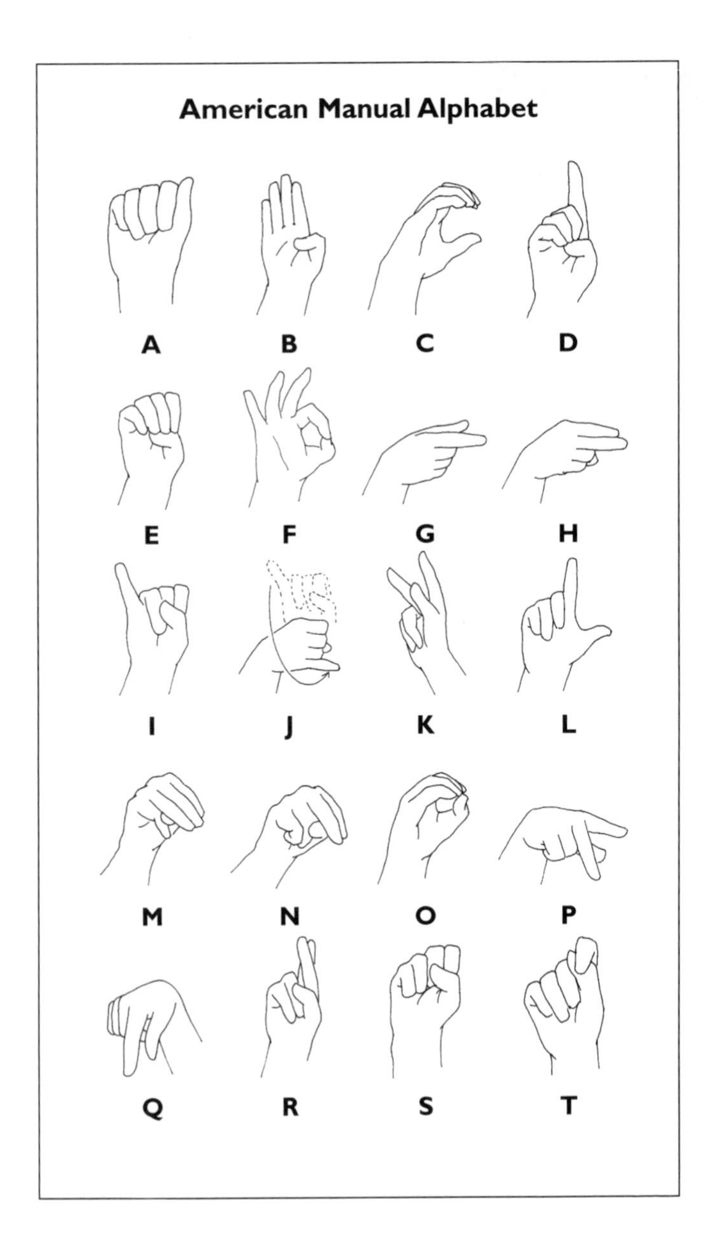
American Manual Alphabet
A
B
C
D
E
F
G
H
I
J
K
L
M
N
O
P
Q
R
S
T

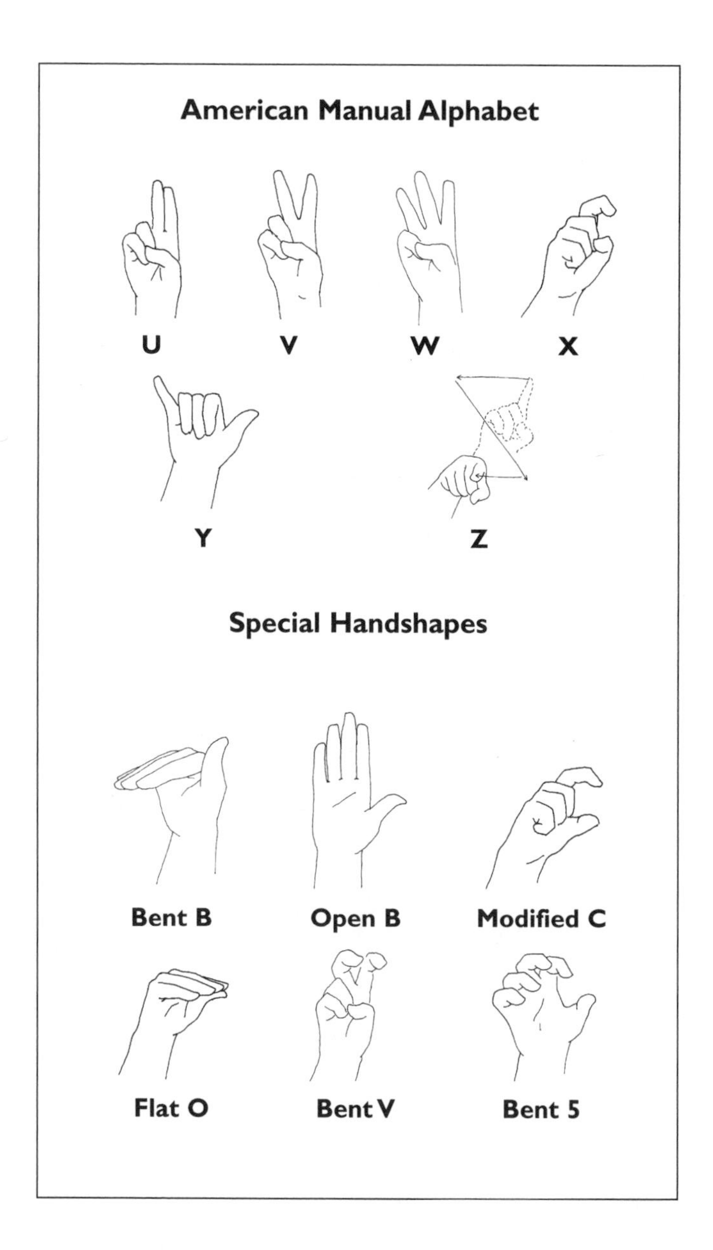
American Manual Alphabet
U
V
W
X
Y
Z
Special Handshapes
Bent B
Open B
Modified C
Flat O
Bent V
Bent 5

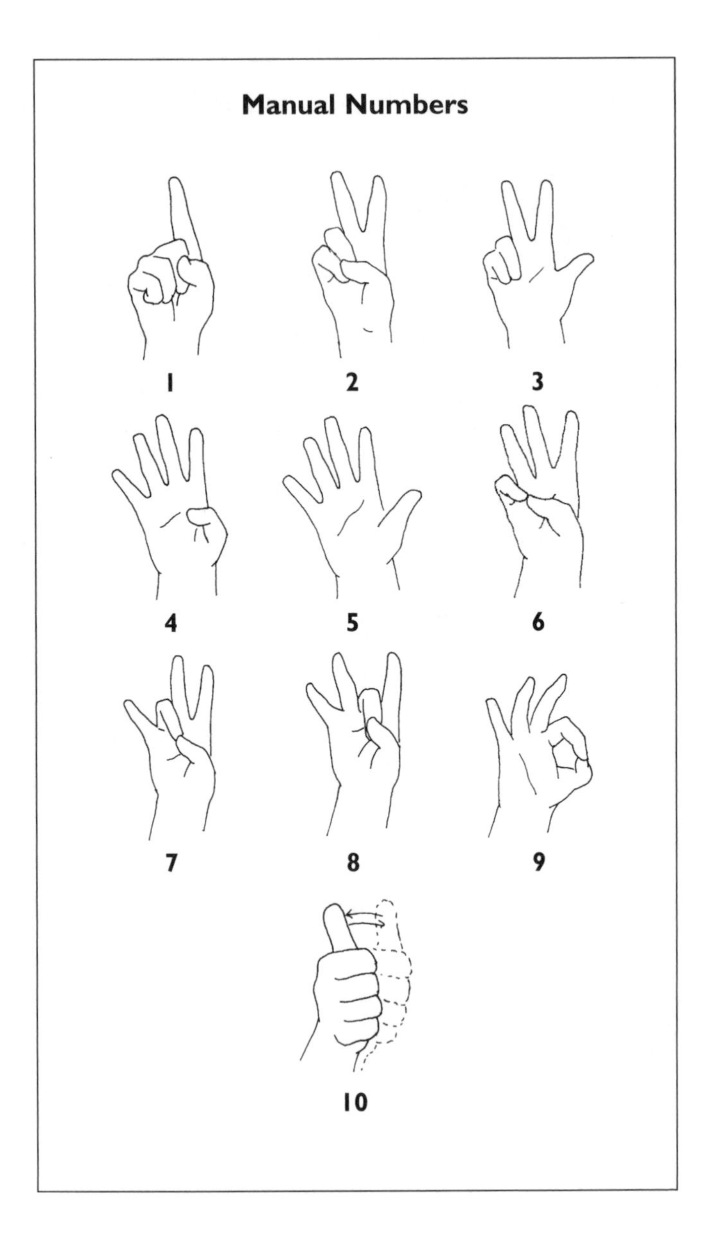
Manual Numbers
1
2
3
4
5
6
7
8
9
10

again, repeat

Hit the palm of the left Open B hand with the fingertips of the Bent B right hand.

Tip: If you are doing an activity and you want to know whether the child wants to do it again, you can sign the word *again* or the word *more* while raising your eyebrows.

---

airplane

Move the right Y hand, with the index finger extended, in small forward movements away from the body.

Memory aid: I love to fly. The handshape resembles the sign for *I love you.*

Tip: Most babies will point their index finger to the sky. This gesture is fine, but remember to keep using the correct sign.

---

all done, finished

Start with both 5 hands palms up, and then flip over the hands.

Memory aid: Imagine food on your hands; you turn your hands over, and the food is all gone.

Tip: This sign is a good one to use at all times, but using it at mealtime is ideal for little ones. The child can sign to you that he or she is done without having to throw food on the floor, and that will be a welcome change.

alligator

Touch the heels of both hands together and snap hands together several times.

Memory aid: The hands resemble the jaws of an alligator opening and closing.

Tip: *Crocodile* is not signed the same way. See *crocodile*.

all right

Place the little-finger edge of the right Open B hand across the palm of the left Open B hand. Slide the right hand up until the fingertips are pointing up.

ambulance, siren

Raise both Bent 5 hands above the shoulders and rotate the hands from side to side.

Memory aid: The hands represent the flashing lights.

angry

Quickly move the right Bent 5 hand from the chest up to the face.

Memory aid: Think of anger rising from the chest to the face.

Tip: Remember to use your facial expression. It will show the true meaning of this sign, especially the type and intensity of the anger you are expressing.

---

animal

Rest the fingertips of both hands on the chest and bend and straighten the fingers a couple of times.

Memory aid: Picture an animal breathing deeply.

---

ant

Slide the thumb of the right A hand off the thumb of the left A hand several times.

Memory aid: The small motion represents the sign for *work* because ants are hard workers.

apple

Place the index finger of the right X hand on the cheek and twist the hand back and forth a couple of times.

Memory aid: An apple a day keeps the dentist away.

aunt

Rub the thumb of the right A hand down the side of the right cheek a couple of times.

Memory aid: The A is the initial letter of *aunt,* and the movement is on the female part of the face.

baby, infant

Place the right hand and forearm on the left hand and forearm and rock the arms side to side.

Memory aid: Imagine rocking a baby in your arms.

baby-sit, take care of (baby + care)

baby: Place the right hand and forearm on the left hand and forearm and rock the arms side to side.

care: Gently tap the right K hand on top of the left K hand a couple of times.

Memory aid: The K hands represent eyes watching over the child. To say *babysitter,* add the sign *person* (see page 123) after *care.*

---

bacon

Start with the tips of both H hands touching and then move the hands apart in a wavy motion.

Memory aid: Picture the way bacon looks while it cooks.

---

bagel

Move both G hands so they form a circle from the chest outward.

Memory aid: Form the shape of a round bagel. The fingers represent the width of the bagel.

ball

With palms facing, tap fingertips and thumbs of both Bent 5 hands several times.

Memory aid: Think about the way you hold a ball.

---

balloon

Place the C hands in front of the mouth, then spread them apart to show the outline of a balloon while, at the same time, puffing out the cheeks.

Memory aid: Envision blowing up a balloon.

Tip: Making your eyes big and wide while blowing up the balloon adds fun expression to the sign.

banana

Point the left index finger up and "peel" it with the right Flat O hand.

Memory aid: Peel a banana.

bandage, band aid

Slide the extended fingers of the right H hand across the back of the left B hand, from the little finger toward the thumb.

Memory aid: Think of applying a bandage to the skin.

---

baseball

Place the right fist on top of the left wrist near the right shoulder and bounce hands back and forth.

Memory aid: Picture a baseball player who is ready to hit the ball with the bat.

---

basketball

With both Bent 5 hands facing each other, bend wrists back and forth a few times.

Memory aid: Mime throwing a basketball toward a basket.

bath

Place both A hands on either side of the chest and rub them up-and-down in small movements.

Memory aid: The motion of the sign represents scrubbing the dirt off of the body.

beach

Flutter the fingers of the right hand toward the left hand and then flutter them back to the original position.

Memory aid: The left hand represents the shore, and the right hand represents the waves approaching and receding from the shore.

bean

Tap the right X finger along the extended left index finger from knuckle to fingertip.

Memory aid: Imagine beans in a pod.

Tip: You can use this sign for a variety of beans.

bear

Cross the arms on the chest and lightly scratch the chest with the fingers of both Bent 5 hands.

Memory aid: Think of a bear hug or of a bear scratching.

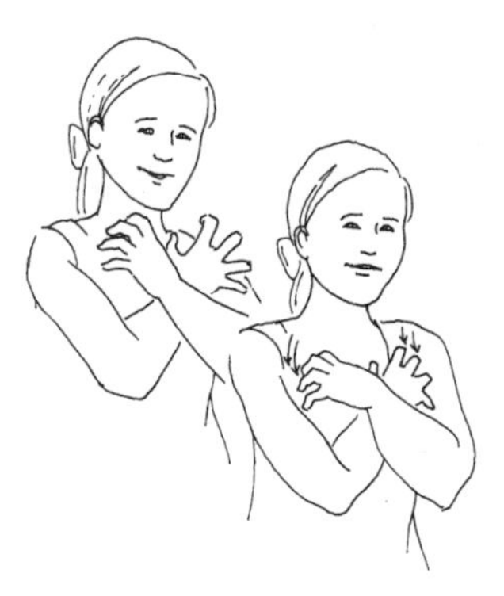

---

beautiful, lovely, pretty

The right 5 hand moves in a circle around the face, ending in a Flat O hand.

Memory aid: Beautiful face.

---

bed

Rest the right cheek against the palm of the right Open B hand and tilt the head slightly toward the hand.

Memory aid: Picture laying your head against a pillow.

Tip: Signers can also use this sign for *night-night, nap,* and *sleep.*

bee, wasp

Put the index finger and thumb of the right F hand on the cheek, then open the hand and quickly brush the cheek.

Memory aid: The bee stings the face and is swatted away.

bell

Hit the palm of the left Open B hand with the right index finger two times.

Memory aid: The index finger represents the clangor of the bell, which hits the inside of the bell.

belt

Place Modified C hands at either side of the waist and bring the hands together.

Memory aid: The motion of the sign represents putting on a belt.

bib

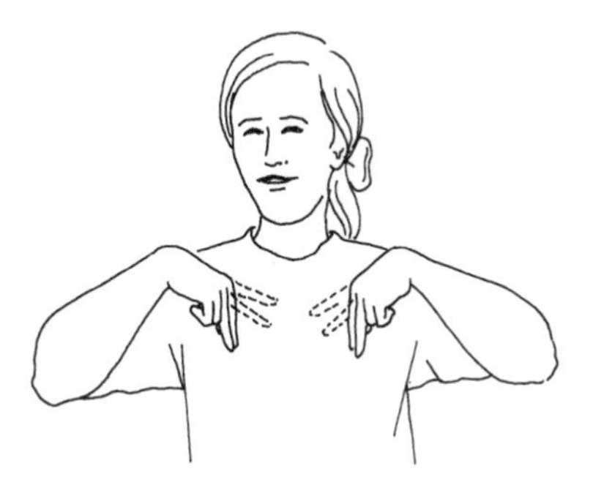

Place thumbs of both 3 hands on the chest and bring index and middle fingers down to thumbs.

Memory aid: Imagine placing a bib on the baby's chest.

---

bicycle, bike, pedal

Move both S hands in forward alternating circles.

Memory aid: Picture the moving pedals of a bike.

Tip: Use this sign also for *ride a bike.*

---

big, large

Start with Open B hands close together, then arc the arms out to either side of the body to show how large the object is.

Tip: How far you spread your arms depends on the size of the object you are describing.

bird

Place the back of the G hand at the mouth and open and close the index finger and thumb.

Memory aid: The fingers represent a bird's beak opening and closing.

birthday (birth + day)

birth: Place the right hand on the chest and move the hand out and down, landing on the left palm.

day: Rest the elbow of the upright right arm on the back of the left hand, and move the right hand (either D hand or Open B hand) down toward the left elbow.

Memory aid: The sign for *birth* represents a baby coming out of the womb to a waiting hand. In the sign for *day,* the right hand represents the sun's travel through the sky during the day.

Tip: There are many different signs for *birthday,* so don't be surprised if you know or see another sign.

bite

Place the right Bent 5 hand slightly above the left Open B hand. Then bring the right hand down and latch the fingertips onto the left hand.

Memory aid: The fingers of the right hand are the teeth that are biting the left hand.

Tip: Be aware of your facial expression. Be firm when you tell your child not to bite. The facial expression will show that you are serious.

black

Brush the right index finger across the forehead from left brow to right brow.

Memory aid: Think of black eyebrows.

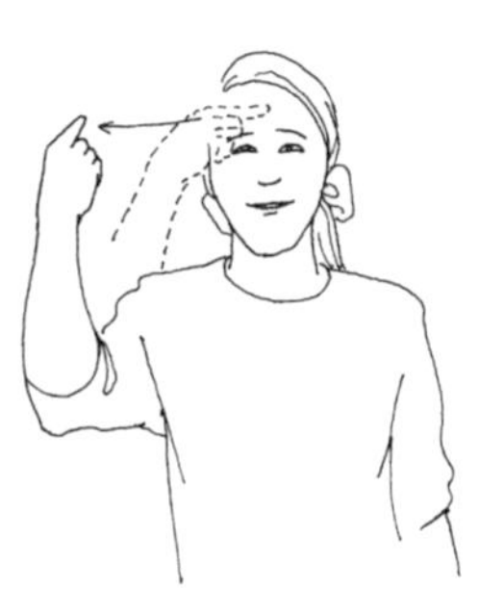

blanket, cover

Position both 5 hands in front of the stomach. Then pull the hands up toward the chest while closing both hands to the Flat O handshape.

Memory aid: Imagine pulling a blanket up to the chin.

blocks

Place the upright right Modified C hand in front of the chest, then turn the hand down, as if stacking one block on top of another.

blue

Twist the right B hand from side to side several times.

Memory aid: The B handshape represents the *B* for *blue.*

boat, ship

Move slightly curved hands, little fingers touching, forward in a wavy, up-and-down motion.

Memory aid: Think of a boat moving in the water.

body

Start with both hands on the chest and move the hands down to the stomach.

bologna, sausage

With C hands side by side, close the C hands to S hands repeatedly while moving hands apart.

Memory aid: The motion of the sign represents meat being pinched into links.

---

book

Place the Open B hands together in front of the body, then open hands until the palms are facing up.

Memory aid: The hands represent the cover of the book, and the palms represent the pages.

---

bottle

Rest the little finger side of the right C hand on the left Open B palm. Raise the right hand straight up as if outlining the shape of the bottle.

Tip: If you are asking what the baby wants, consider signing the contents of the bottle (for example, *milk* or *juice*) instead of signing *bottle*. This approach makes communication easier during the transition from bottle to cup because the child who wants milk, juice, or water will sign *milk, juice,* or *water,* which is clearer than the sign *bottle.*

bowl

Position both slightly curved hands together in front of the body so little fingers are touching. Curve the hands up and apart until the palms are facing each other.

Memory aid: Create the shape of the bowl.

Tip: The distance between your hands shows the size of the bowl. If the bowl is small, the hands will be close together. If the bowl is large, the hands will be farther apart.

boy

Open and close the right Flat O hand a couple of times at the right side of the forehead.

Memory aid: Think of a boy adjusting the brim of his baseball cap.

bread

Use the fingertips of the right Bent B hand to slice down the back of the left hand.

Memory aid: The motions of this sign represent slicing a loaf of bread.

break, broke, broken

Place S hands side by side in front of the body and then sharply move them apart and upward.

Memory aid: Imagine grasping a stick and breaking it in two.

---

breakfast (eat + morning)

eat: Bring the fingertips of the Flat O hand up to the lips.

morning: Place the left hand in the crook of the right elbow and raise the right forearm up.

Memory aid: In the sign morning, the left arm represents the horizon, and the raising of the right hand represents the sun coming up.

---

brother

Touch the right temple with the thumb of the right L hand and then move the hand down to rest on the left L hand.

Memory aid: The sign begins on the temple, which is the male part of the face.

brown

Place the index finger of the right B hand on the cheek and slide the hand down.

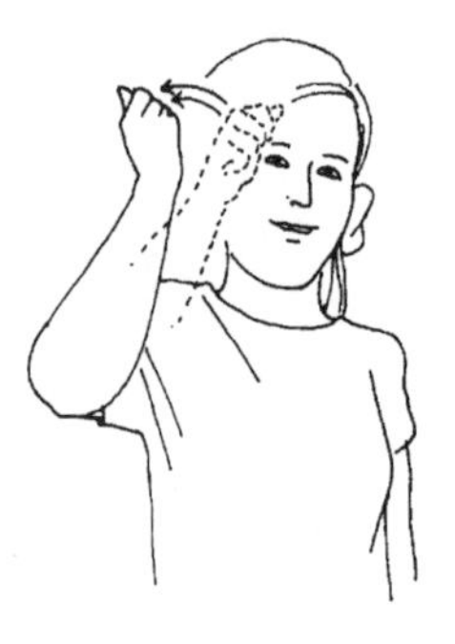

brush

Grasp an imaginary brush and run it through the hair.

Memory aid: Mime brushing the hair.

brush teeth, toothbrush

Move the index finger of the right hand up and down in front of the teeth.

Memory aid: Use your finger as an imaginary toothbrush.

bubbles

Flutter the fingers of both 5 hands while raising both hands up from the waist to the neck.

Memory aid: Think of bubbles floating up into the air.

Tip: You can use this sign for bath bubbles.

buckle

Hold both modified C hands palms down at the waist. Bring both hands around to the front of the body and touch together.

Memory aid: Wrap a belt around the waist and fasten the buckle.

bug, insect

Put the thumb of the right 3 hand on the nose. Bend the index and middle fingers up and down a few times.

Memory aid: The fingers represent the antennas moving.

bus

Place the little finger of the right B hand on the index finger of the left B hand and tap the hands together several times.

Memory aid: The hands show the length of the bus, and the B handshapes will help you remember the *B* in *bus*.

butter, margarine

Slide the fingers of the right H hand off the heel of the left palm.

Memory aid: Pretend that you are spreading butter on bread.

butterfly

Hook the thumbs of both Open B hands and flutter both hands.

Memory aid: The hands represent the wings of the butterfly.

button

Place the thumb and index finger of the right F on the chest and tap down the front of the body, showing where the buttons on a shirt are located.

cake

Slide the fingertips of the right C hand down the palm of the left Open B hand, from the wrist to the fingertips.

Memory aid: The sign mimics slicing a piece of cake.

camel

Outline the shape of a camel's two humps using the Bent B right hand.

camera

Hold an imaginary camera up to the eyes. Bounce the right index finger up and down a few times, as if you are pushing down the shutter button.

Memory aid: The sign mimics the action of taking a photograph.

Tip: You can use this sign also for *take a picture.*

camp

Begin with the extended index and little fingers of both hands touching, then pull the hands down while bending the index and little fingers and repeat.

Memory aid: The hands are in the shape of a tent.

candy

Twist the right index finger on the cheek.

Memory aid: Think of pointing to your sweet tooth.

Safety tip: Remember not to call medicine *candy* to your children.

car, auto, vehicle

Move both S hands alternately up and down in front of the body.

Memory tip: Mimic holding on to the steering wheel.

---

careful

Place the right K hand on top of the left K hand and gently tap the two hands against each other several times.

Memory aid: Think of the fingers as eyes keeping watch over something or someone.

---

carrot

Place the right S hand near the mouth and twist the hand forward as if eating a carrot.

cat

Start with the right F hand on the cheek and pull the hand away as if stroking a whisker.

Tip: Cat can also be signed with two hands. ASL has another sign for *kitten,* but the sign *cat* may be used for *kitten.*

catch

With Bent 5 hands positioned at each shoulder, bring the hands down and together in front of the body as though catching a ball.

caterpillar

Bend and extend the right index finger while moving the right hand up the left arm.

Memory aid: Picture a caterpillar crawling up your arm.

celery

Bring the right C hand up and through the left C hand while twisting the right arm slightly.

Memory aid: The sign represents celery growing.

---

cereal

Position the fingertips of the right C hand on the chin and move the whole hand up in small, repeated movements.

Memory aid: Think of moving your hand to your mouth as if you were eating cereal.

---

chair

Tap the bent extended fingers of the right H hand on the extended fingers of the left H hand twice.

Memory aid: The fingers of the right hand represent the legs when sitting on a chair.

Tip: sit is very similar to the sign chair. The only difference is that chair has repeated movement (see the description for *sit*).

chalk

Use your hand to hold an imaginary piece of chalk and write in the air on an imaginary chalkboard.

change

Place the right X hand on top of the left X hand and swing the hands around to reverse the hand positions.

cheese

Press the heel of the right hand into the heel of the left hand and twist the right hand slightly left and right.

Memory aid: The sign is based on the action of shaping cheese.

chicken

Move the right X hand from the nose to the upturned left palm, then scratch the left palm several times.

Memory aid: Imagine a chicken pecking at feed on the ground.

Tip: This sign can be used to refer to the animal or to the food.

---

children, kids

Begin with both Open B hands in front of the body. Then, move the hands apart in small bouncing motions.

Memory aid: Picture the hands tapping the top of each child's head in a row.

---

chocolate

Sit the right C hand on the back of the left Open B hand and move the right hand in small circles.

Memory aid: Imagine stirring melted chocolate.

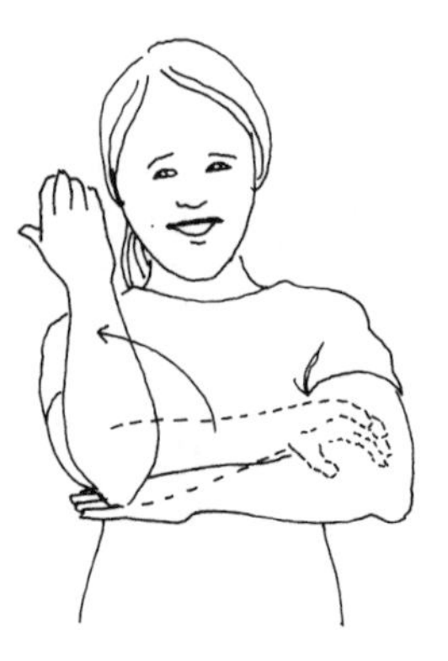

Christmas

Rest the right elbow and forearm on the left forearm in front of the body. Keeping the right elbow in position, raise the right arm to an upright position, slowly twisting the C hand toward the body.

Memory aid: The C hand is outlining the arch of a wreath.

church

Tap the right C hand on the back of the left S hand.

Memory aid: The C represents the church, standing on a solid foundation.

circle

Draw the shape of a circle in the air with the index finger.

class

Start with the thumbs and index fingers of the C hands touching in front of the body and then move the hands outward in a circle until the little fingers meet.

Memory aid: The C hands, representing *class,* form a group.

Tip: Group can be signed the same way or with G hands.

---

clay, play-dough

Using Bent 5 hands facing each other, twist the hands alternately toward and away from the body.

Memory aid: The action of the sign represents molding the clay.

---

clean

Slide the right Open B hand down the left Open B palm a couple of times.

Memory aid: Picture wiping off a plate with your hand.

close, shut

With palms of both B hands facing up on either side of the body, turn the hands over until the index fingers touch.

Memory aid: Closing a box.

close-to, near, neighbor

Place both Bent B hands in front of the body, the right hand in front of the left hand. Move the right hand back until it touches the left palm.

Memory aid: The movement of the right hand indicates moving closer to an object.

closet

Hook the index finger of the right X hand over the left index finger several times.

Memory aid: Envision hanging hangers on the closet rod.

clothes

Brush the thumbs of both 5 hands down the chest several times.

Memory aid: The motion represents smoothing out clothes on your body.

---

clown, circus

Touch the tip of the nose with the fingers of the right Bent 5 hand.

Memory aid: Think of a big red clown nose.

---

coat, jacket

Rub the thumbs of both Y hands down the shoulders to the chest.

Memory aid: The hands outline an imaginary lapel.

Tip: You can use this sign to tell your child to put on his or her jacket.

cold (sick)

Grab the nose with the index finger and thumb and slide the hand down several times.

Memory aid: Think of a runny nose.

cold (temperature), chilly

Position both S hands at shoulder level and shake the hands back and forth slightly.

Memory aid: The sign represents the body shaking from the cold air.

color (noun)

Place the fingertips of the right 5 hand on the chin and wiggle the fingers.

Memory aid: The fingers represent the colors of the rainbow.

color (verb)

Move the fingertips of the right Flat O hand down the left palm in a zigzag movement.

Memory aid: Think of coloring on a piece of paper.

---

comb

Use the fingertips of the right Bent 5 hand to "comb" from the front of the head to the back of the head.

Memory aid: The fingers represent the teeth of the comb.

---

come, come here

Arc the right index finger of the upright right hand toward the body.

Memory aid: Point to a person and tell them to come to you.

computer

Move the right C hand in small circles down the extended left arm, starting at the shoulder and ending at the wrist.

Tip: Some people sign computer in the same way but with an H hand.

cook

Lay the right Open B hand on the left palm, and then flip the right hand over.

Memory aid: Think of flipping a pancake or turning over food in a frying pan.

cookie

Place the fingertips of the right Bent 5 hand on the left Open B palm, then bounce and twist the right hand, landing on the left palm again.

Memory aid: Envision the action of cutting cookie dough with a cookie cutter.

corn, corn-on-the-cob

Hold an imaginary piece of corn with both hands in front of the mouth and move the hands from side to side. Open and close your teeth several times as if taking bites from the corn.

---

couch

Slide the fingers of the right H hand down the extended fingers of the left H hand.

Memory aid: The right fingers represent legs moving along the length of the couch.

---

count

Move the thumb and index finger of the right F hand along the palm of the left Open B hand, starting from palm and moving toward the fingertips.

Memory aid: Imagine moving beads on an old-fashioned counting board, or abacus.

cow

Rest the thumbs of both Y hands on the temples and twist the hands back and forth several times.

Memory aid: Picture a cow's horns.

Tip: Be sure to moo when signing *cow.* The child can then associate the sound with the animal and the sign.

crab

Hold both G hands out in front of the body and open and close the index fingers and thumbs twice.

Memory aid: Picture the crab's claws opening and closing.

cracker

Hit the left elbow with the right S hand several times.

Memory aid: Long ago, bakers would bake thin bread and crack it on their elbow to break it into pieces called crackers.

crayon, (color [noun] + draw)

color: Place the fingertips of the right 5 hand on the chin and wiggle the fingers.

draw: Place the index finger and thumb of the right Baby O hand on the fingertips of the left Open B hand and "draw" down the left palm.

Memory aid: The left hand represents a piece of paper and the right hand is the crayon.

Tip: See page 56 for an alternate way to sign *draw*.

---

crib (baby + bed)

baby: Place the right hand and forearm on the left hand and forearm and rock the arms side to side.

bed: Rest your cheek on the palm of your right hand.

Tip: When you talk to an adult about a crib, you can fingerspell c-r-i-b instead of signing it.

---

crocodile

With heels of both Bent 5 hands touching, open and close the hands a few times.

Memory aid: Picture the mouth of the crocodile opening and closing.

Tip: *Alligator* has a slightly different sign. See page 14.

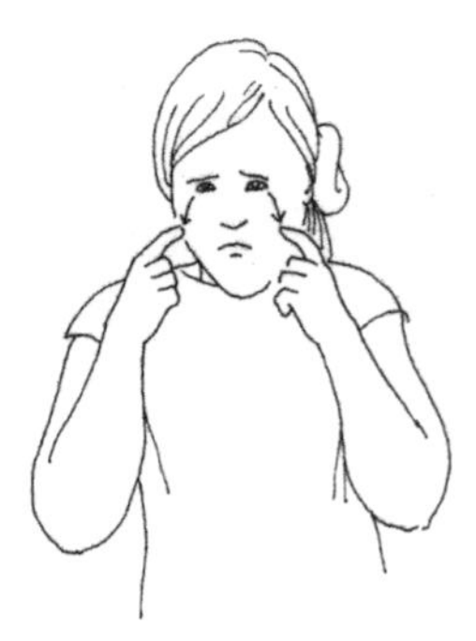

cry

Slide both index fingers down the cheeks.

Memory aid: The fingers trace tears falling down the cheeks.

Tip: You can also make this sign using only one finger. Be sure to use a sad facial expression when signing this word so the child understands the true meaning of the word.

cup

Place the right C hand on the palm of the left Open B hand.

Memory aid: Show the shape of a cup.

cupcake

Place the fingertips of the right Bent 5 hand on the palm of the left Open B hand. Raise the right hand up about two inches and repeat.

Memory aid: Think of a small cake rising.

cute

Gently brush the fingertips of the right H hand down the chin several times.

Tip: Many people sign this with the thumb extended.

---

dance

Swing the fingertips of the right V hand back and forth above the palm of the left Open B hand.

Memory aid: The fingers represent dancing legs.

---

dark

Swing the upright 5 hands across the face and down.

Memory aid: Think of shutting out the light.

day

Rest the elbow of the upright right arm on the back of the left hand, and move the right D hand down toward the left elbow.

Memory aid: Picture the sun going across the sky from noon to night.

deer

Rest the thumbs of both 5 hands on the temples.

Memory aid: Make the deer's antlers.

diaper

Rest the thumbs on either side of the waist, and then bring the index and middle fingers down to the thumbs twice.

Memory aid: Think of closing the tabs of a disposable diaper.

dinner, supper

Tap the lips several times with the thumb and fingers of the right D hand.

Memory aid: Eat the D for dinner.

---

dinosaur

Bounce the right D hand up the extended left arm.

Memory aid: The right hand outlines the humps on the back and neck of the dinosaur.

---

dirty, messy

Place the back of the right 5 hand under the chin and wiggle the fingers.

Memory aid: This sign is similar to the sign for *pig,* which is a messy animal. (See *pig.*)

doctor

Tap the fingers of the right M hand on the inside of the left wrist several times.

Memory aid: Think of taking the pulse on the wrist. The *M* represents M.D.

dog

Pat your thigh several times, as if calling a dog to come.

Tip: The sign also can be made by snapping the fingers and then patting the leg.

doll

Brush the right X finger down the nose two times.

Memory aid: Dolls have cute noses.

dolphin

Move the right D hand in small up-and-down wavy motions.

Memory aid: Visualize a dolphin diving in and out of the surface of the water.

---

donkey

Rest the thumbs of both Open B hands on the temples and then bend the fingers down a few times.

Memory aid: Picture the ears of the donkey flapping.

Tip: The donkey sign is similar to the sign for *stubborn* (which is usually made with one hand and the fingers bend only once) because the donkey can be a stubborn animal.

---

door

Position both B hands together in front of the chest, and then twist the right hand back and forth two times.

Memory aid: The door is opening and closing.

doughnut

Starting with both R hands at the lips, circle the hands away from the body until the fingertips of both hands touch.

Memory aid: Make a ring in the shape of a doughnut.

down

Move the right hand, with the index finger pointing down, from above the shoulder down to the waist.

Memory aid: Show the down motion.

draw, art

Using the little finger of the right hand, "draw" down the palm of the left hand.

Memory aid: The little finger represents a pencil drawing on a piece of paper.

drink

Touch the lips with the thumb of the C hand and tilt the wrist up.

Memory aid: The sign mimics taking a drink from a glass or a cup.

drive

Position both S hands at shoulder level and move them out and away from the body.

Memory aid: Imagine driving from here to there.

drum

Alternately move both A hands up and down in front of the body.

Memory aid: Imagine holding drums sticks and playing an imaginary drum.

duck

Place the back of the right hand at the mouth and open and close the index and middle fingers on the thumb.

Memory aid: Think of the duck's bill opening and closing.

Tip: Make the quack-quack sound while signing this word to add some fun for the children and to help them learn the sound that the duck makes.

eagle, hawk

Tap the tip of the nose a few times with the back of the right X finger.

Memory aid: The X finger represents the eagle's hooked beak.

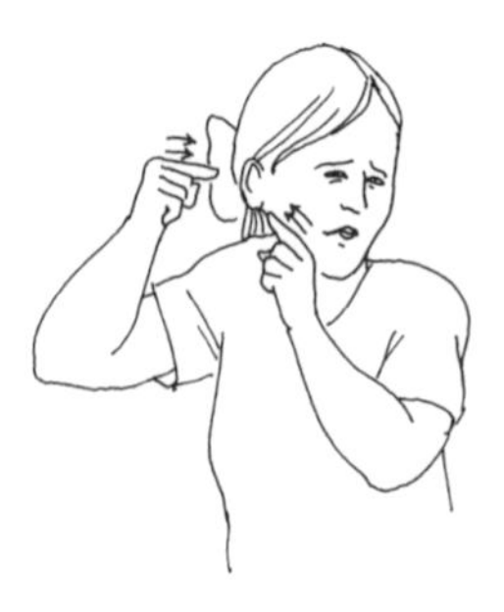

earache

Place the extended index fingers in front of the right ear and slide the hands toward each other two times.

Tip: Many children will simply stick their finger in their ear to let you know that it hurts, but continue to teach *earache*. This sign actually is the sign *hurt* in front of the ear. See *hurt* for additional information.

early

Slide the right middle finger across the back of the left Open B hand.

Easter

Twist the right E hand back and forth two times.

eat, snack

Touch the lips with the fingertips of the Flat O hand.

Memory aid: Think of placing food in your mouth.

Tip: If you want to ask the child whether he or she is hungry or wants to eat, you can use this sign while raising your eyebrows (to show a question).

egg

Place the fingers of the right H hand on the fingers of the left H hand and twist the hands apart and down.

Memory aid: Picture the eggshell breaking and the egg coming out.

elephant

Position the Open B right hand on the nose and move it down in the shape of an elephant's trunk.

Memory aid: Think of the long trunk.

Tip: As with signs for other animals, make an elephant sound when signing elephant to add some fun and to link the sound and the sign.

excited, thrilled

Alternately touch the middle fingers of the 5 hands on the chest and circle them around.

Memory aid: The heart is beating rapidly from excitement.

Tip: Make a very excited face to show the true meaning of the word.

eyes

Point to one eye and then the other.

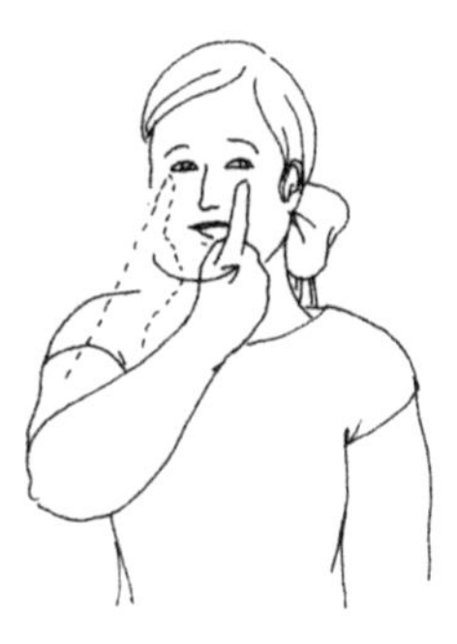

---

face

Move the right index finger in a circle around the face.

Tip: You can use this sign with a questioning look on your face when asking, What does it look like?

---

fair, equal, even

Tap together the fingertips of both Bent B hands several times.

Memory aid: The hands are even to show equality.

fall down

Stand the fingertips of the right V hand on the palm of the left Open B hand. Then flip the V over so the back of the hand lands on the left palm.

Memory aid: Picture a person standing and then falling down.

family

Start with the thumbs and index fingers of the F hands touching in front of the body and then move the hands outward in a circle until the little fingers meet.

Memory aid: Think of a family circle.

farm

Brush the thumb of the right 5 hand along the chin, from one cheek to the other.

Tip: Remember to use this sign for the song "Old MacDonald Had a Farm."

fast, speed

Point both index fingers of the L hands out and then quickly jerk the hands back while bending the index fingers.

father, daddy

Tap the forehead with the thumb of the right 5 hand.

Memory aid: The sign is made on the male part of the face.

Tip: This sign also can be made by placing the thumb of the right 5 hand on the forehead and wiggling the fingers.

feel (verb), feelings (noun)

Place the middle finger of the right 5 hand on the chest and brush the finger up.

Memory aid: The motion of the sign shows emotions flowing upward.

fever, temperature

sick: Touch the middle of the forehead with the middle finger of the right 5 hand.

temperature: The horizontal right index finger slides up and down the left index finger, showing the temperature rising in the thermometer.

Memory aid: The head is getting hot.

find

Position the right F hand below the left Bent 5 hand and pull the right hand out and above the left hand.

Memory aid: Envision finding something and picking it up.

fire

Start with both 5 hands at the waist and move the hands up while fluttering the fingers.

Memory aid: The hands resemble flames.

firefighter

Tap the top of the forehead with the thumb of the right Modified C hand.

Memory aid: The sign represents the shield on the front of the helmet.

---

fire truck (firefighter + ambulance)

firefighter: Tap the top of the forehead with the thumb of the right Modified C hand.

ambulance: Raise both Bent 5 hands above the shoulders and rotate the hands from side to side.

Memory tip: The moving hands imitate the ambulance lights.

---

fish

Wiggle the right Open B hand forward as if it were a fish swimming.

Memory aid: The hand represents a fish swimming in the water.

Tip: You can use this sign for all types of fish as well as for food.

flag

Rest the heel of the right Open B hand on the index finger of the left 1 hand and bend the right hand back and forth.

Memory tip: The hand waves like a flag.

---

flower

Touch the right side of the nose with the right Flat O hand, and then touch the left side of the nose.

Memory aid: Imagine smelling a flower.

Tip: Don't be surprised if your child signs *flower* by placing one finger straight up a nostril. Be sure to use the right sign without correcting your child.

fly (like an airplane)

Move the Y hand with the index finger extended forward as if your hand were a plane taking off.

Memory aid: I love to fly, and the handshape is the same one used to sign *I love you.*

Tip: The handshape for this sign is the same as the one for airplane, but the movement is a little different. (See *airplane.*)

fly (like a bird)

Extend both arms out to the side of the body and flap the hands up and down.

Memory aid: The arms and hands flap like a bird's wings.

---

fly (insect)

Make an F hand and wiggle it around in a circle, like a flying insect.

Memory aid: Picture a fly buzzing around.

Tip: You can use this sign for any type of flying insect.

---

food

Touch the lips with the fingertips of the Flat O hand two times.

Memory aid: Imagine putting food in your mouth.

Tip: This is similar to the same sign for *eat* and *snack,* except for the double movement.

football

Using 5 hands, interlock the fingers of both hands and then pull the hands apart several times.

Memory aid: Envision the bodily contact the teams have.

forest

Rest the elbow of the right arm on the back of the left hand. Move the arms to the right while twisting the right arm and 5 hand from side to side.

Memory aid: Picture a series of trees on land.

Tip: This sign also can be made without using the left arm.

fork

Jab the fingertips of the right V hand into the palm of the left Open B hand.

Memory aid: The fork is stabbing a piece of food.

fox

Place the right F hand in front of the nose and bend the wrist down two times.

Memory aid: The sign refers to a fox's pointed nose.

---

french fries

Swing the right F hand from left to right a couple of times.

Memory aid: Think of dipping French fries.

---

friend

Hook the right index finger in the crook of the left index finger, then reverse the hands and hook the left finger in the crook of the right finger.

Memory aid: Think of being locked together in friendship.

frog

Start with the right S hand under the chin and then quickly flick out the index and middle fingers twice.

Memory aid: The sign imitates the frog's legs kicking.

---

fruit

Place the index finger and thumb of the right F hand on the cheek and twist the wrist.

Memory aid: Twist a piece of fruit off of the stem.

frustrated (adjective), frustration (noun)

Quickly bring up the back of the right B hand to the nose and mouth area. The head can move back slightly.

Memory aid: Imagine a door shutting in your face.

fun

Touch the nose with the extended fingers of the right H hand and then move the hand down to touch the back of the fingers of the left H hand.

Memory aid: Remember that the nose wrinkles when people laugh.

---

funny

Touch the tip of the nose with the extended fingertips of the right H hand and then slide the fingers off the tip of the nose, bending them slightly. Repeat this movement several times.

Memory aid: People wrinkle their noses when they laugh.

Tip: Many people sign this with the thumb extended.

---

game

Bring A hands together and tap knuckles several times.

Memory aid: The hands represent people competing against each other.

get

Place the right Bent 5 hand above the left Bent 5 hand and then move the hands toward the body, closing the hands and ending with the right hand on top of the left hand.

Memory aid: Grasp something and bring it to the body.

Tip: The sign can be made using only one hand.

giraffe

Position the C hand at the front of the neck and raise the hand up to outline the long neck of a giraffe.

Tip: Some children might use one finger and either point to the neck or run a finger up their neck, but continue to use the correct sign with the child.

girl

Gently stroke the thumb of the right A hand down the side of the right cheek two times.

Memory aid: The thumb outlines the string of an old-fashioned bonnet.

Tip: Signs for females are signed on the lower part of the face.

give

Start with the right Flat O hand on the chest and flip the hand over and out as if you were giving a gift to someone.

Memory aid: Giving starts with yourself and is presented to another.

Tip: You also can make this sign with two hands. If you are telling a child to give the item to someone else, you would point your Flat O hand at the child and then move it toward the other person.

---

glass

Tap the front teeth with the tip of the index finger.

Memory aid: Teeth represent something fragile like glass.

---

glasses

Position the G hand near the eye and close the index finger and the thumb while pulling the hand away from the face.

Memory aid: The sign indicates the frame of the glasses.

glue

Move the right G hand from the left side of the mouth to the right side while opening and closing the index finger and thumb to show the stickiness.

Memory aid: Glue is wet (like the mouth) and tacky. You might also think of moistening the glue on an envelope.

go

Bend both upright 1 hands so index fingers point out in the direction you want to go.

Tip: To say "Go to your room," you would move your hands in the direction of the appropriate room.

goat

Move the right S hand from the chin up to the forehead while changing to a Bent V hand.

Memory aid: The S represents the beard and the V represents the horns of a goat.

God

Start with the Open B hand slightly above the head and the fingers pointing forward, then arc the hand down toward the mouth until the fingers are pointing straight up. The signer also can look up while signing.

Memory aid: The One above or the God in heaven.

---

good

Touch the mouth with the fingertips of the Open B hand, then move the hand out and down to the palm of the left Open B hand.

Memory aid: Taste something, like it, and give it to another.

Tip: This sign looks similar to the sign for *thank you,* which is made with only one hand.

---

goose

Place the back of the Flat O hand on the mouth and then open and close the fingers and thumb.

Memory aid: Think of the beak of the goose.

Tip: Notice the slight difference between this sign and the one for *duck.* You can emphasize this difference by making the honk, honk sound to go with the *goose* sign.

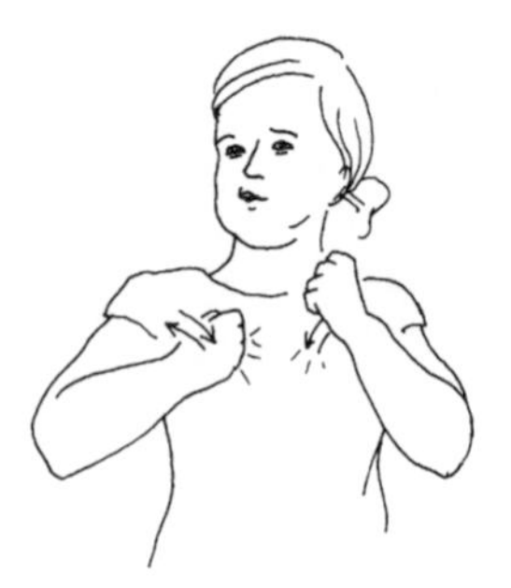

gorilla

Alternately beat both S hands on the chest.

Tip: Add some fun by making the gorilla noise and face as you sign *gorilla.*

grandfather

Position the thumb of the right 5 hand on the forehead and move the hand out in two small arches.

Memory aid: Each arch represents a generation. To indicate a great-grandfather, you would use three arches.

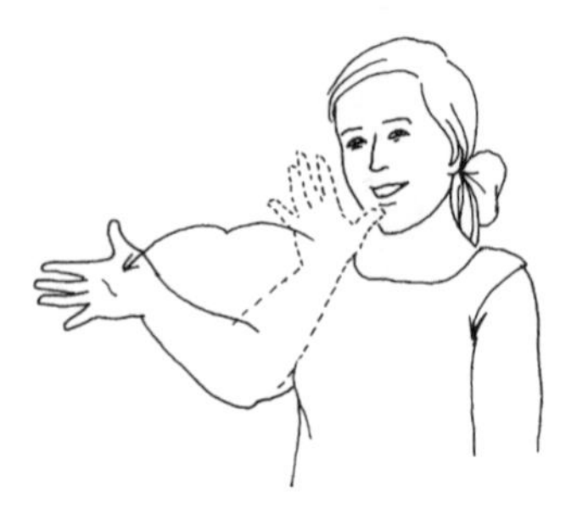

grandmother

Position the thumb of the right 5 hand on the chin and move the hand out in two small arches.

Memory aid: Each arch represents a generation. To indicate a great-grandmother, you would use three arches.

grapes

Tap the fingertips of the right Bent 5 hand down the back of the left hand, moving from the wrist to the fingers.

Memory aid: The movement describes a bunch of grapes.

---

grass

Rub the heel of the right Bent 5 hand against the bottom of the chin a few times.

Memory aid: Imagine trying to see through the blades of growing grass.

---

green

Twist the right G hand from side to side several times.

gum

Bend the fingertips of the right Bent V hand against the cheek several times.

Memory aid: Picture the motion of the cheeks while chewing gum.

---

hair

Pinch a piece of hair between the thumb and index finger of the right F hand.

Memory aid: Show a piece of hair.

Halloween

Position both V hands at the eyes, and then move the hands out while closing the V fingers.

Memory aid: Think of a mask.

hamburger

Clasp the hands together, and then separate them and swing them around to reverse the hand positions.

Memory aid: Imagine shaping hamburger patties.

Tip: For *cheeseburger,* first sign *cheese* and then *hamburger.*

---

hammer

Swing the right X hand, with the thumb tucked inside the index finger, up and down as if you were hitting a nail with a hammer.

---

hands

Brush the back of the Open B right hand down the palm of the left Open B hand, and then reverse the hands and repeat with the movement.

Memory aid: The sign indicates that the hands are separate from the arms.

Hanukkah

Begin with both 4 hands side by side in front of the body and then swing the hands away from each other.

Memory aid: The fingers represent the candles on the menorah.

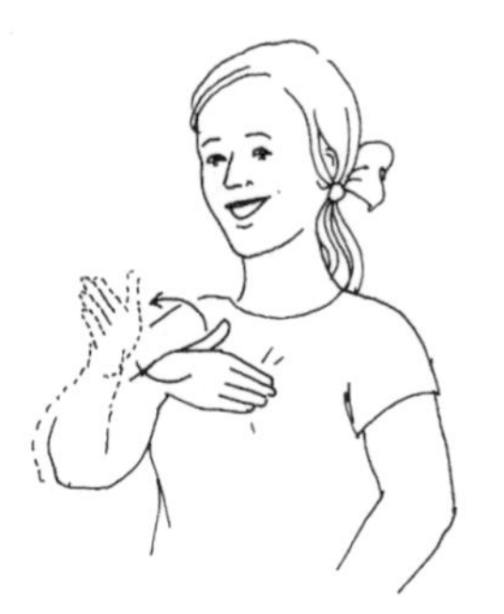

happy

The fingertips of the Open B hand brush the chest in small upward motions several times.

Memory aid: The movement shows happiness rising from the chest.

hard, difficult

Bring the right Bent V hand down on top of the of the left Bent V hand.

Memory aid: The motion of the sign resembles the motion involved in work because doing something that is difficult involves hard work.

hard, solid

Knock the back of the left S hand with the right S hand several times.

Memory aid: Think of something hitting a hard surface.

---

hat

Pat the top of the head with the right Open B hand.

Memory aid: Show the location of the hat on the head.

---

head

Using the fingertips of the right Bent B hand, touch the temple and then move down and touch the lower cheek.

headache

Place the extended index fingers in front of the forehead and slide the index fingers toward each other several times.

Memory aid: Think of the stabbing pain of a headache. (Also remember that you are using the hurt sign to show where the pain is.)

Tip: Be sure to use facial expressions so the child knows the level of pain that is being felt.

hear

Tap the ear several times with the right index finger.

Tip: When you hear a plane fly over, ask the child what he or she hears (what hear?). If the noise is loud enough, the child may either hear or feel the sound and will either sign plane or point up to it.

heart (organ)

Place the middle finger of the right 5 hand on the heart.

Memory aid: You are feeling for a heartbeat.

Tip: Use this sign when you are talking about the actual organ.

heart, valentine (emotion)

Trace the shape of a heart on your chest using the middle fingers of both 5 hands.

Tip: This sign is used for the emotional representation of the heart.

---

helicopter

Rest the right hand top of the left index finger and rock the right hand from side to side.

Memory aid: The blades of the helicopter are moving.

Tip: Be sure that your left index finger is vertical. If it is horizontal, the sign means *fan* or *propeller.*

---

hello

Start with the fingertips of the right hand on the forehead, above the right eyebrow, and move the hand forward.

Memory aid: Think of a salute.

help

Bring the left hand up to meet the right S hand and raise both hands.

Memory aid: Visualize helping someone get up.

Tip: This sign may be difficult for little ones to make at first. Be alert to their attempts at making the sign.

hide

Place the thumb of the right A hand on the mouth and then move it down to "hide" under the palm of the left Bent B hand.

Memory aid: One hand is hiding under the other.

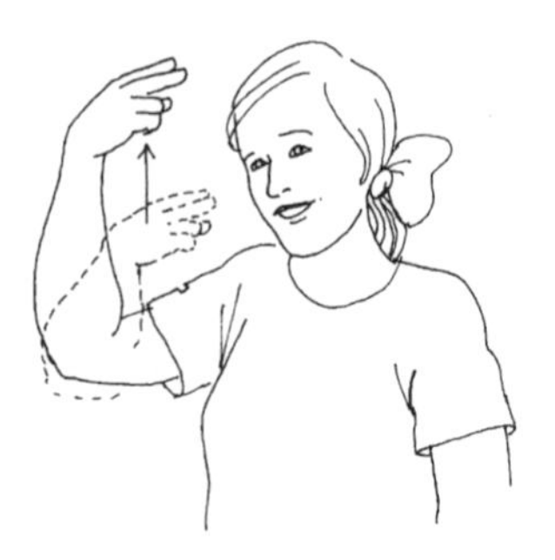

high

Move the H hand from the chest straight up to the top of the head.

Memory aid: Think of going from one level to a higher level.

hippo

Place the right Y hand on top of the left Y hand and tap the thumbs and little fingers of a couple of times.

Memory aid: Imagine the hippo opening and closing its wide mouth, revealing its four prominent teeth.

---

hit

Punch the extended index finger of the left hand with the right S hand.

Memory aid: Envision hitting a person.

---

home

Touch the side of the mouth with the fingertips of the Flat O hand, and then move the hand up and touch the side of the face.

Memory aid: Home is where you eat and sleep.

horse

Place the thumb of the right H hand on the right temple and bend the extended fingers down a few times.

Memory aid: Think of a horse's ear.

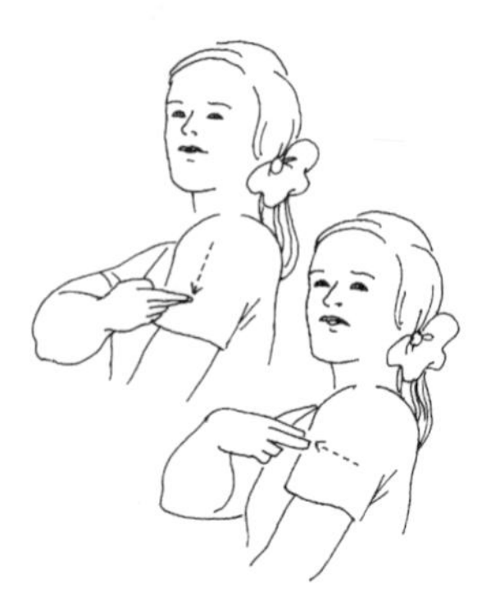

hospital

Trace a cross with the right H hand on the left shoulder.

Memory aid: The sign represents the symbol of the Red Cross.

hot

Start with the Bent 5 hand facing the open mouth, and then quickly drop the hand and flip it over.

Memory aid: Imagine removing hot food from your mouth and throwing it onto the ground.

Tip: Be sure to use your stern facial expression to let your child know that you are very serious.

hot dog

Lay the right index finger down into the left Bent B palm.

Memory aid: Think of placing the hot dog in a bun.

---

house

Touch the thumbs of both Bent B hands together at chin level. Move the hands apart in a downward diagonal line, and then straighten the fingers and bring both hands down about a foot.

Memory aid: The hands outline the shape of the roof and the sides of the house.

---

how

Position the hands in front of the body with the index fingers touching. Then swing the hands around until the fingers are pointing up.

Memory aid: The turning of the palms toward the signer represents revealing the "answer" to how something is done.

how are you?

how: Position the hands in front of the body with the index fingers touching. Then swing the hands around until the fingers are pointing up.

you: Point the index finger at the person to whom you are referring.

Tip: Remember to use a questioning facial expression.

hug

Cross the arms over the chest, raise the shoulders, and twist the torso a little from side to side.

Memory aid: Give yourself a hug.

Tip: To indicate a big hug, you can modify the sign so you cross and wrap your arms around more of your body.

hungry

Move the right Bent 5 hand straight down from the throat to the chest.

Memory aid: Think of food traveling from the throat down to the stomach.

hurry

Twist the H hands alternately up and down.

Memory aid: Imagine someone moving quickly.

hurt

Tap the tips of both index fingers together several times. Place the hands in the area that is feeling the pain.

Memory aid: Think of stabbing pain.

Tip: The sign for *hurt* is always made next to the area that hurts. For example, *headache* is signed at the forehead, and *toothache* is signed in front of the mouth.

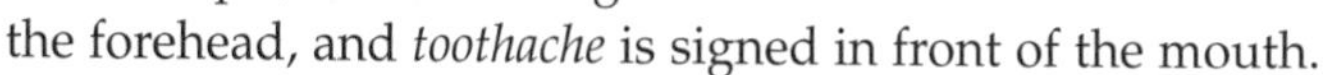

ice cream

Position the S hand near the chin and make small circles toward the mouth.

Memory aid: The motion of the sign mimics licking an ice-cream cone.

Tip: You can stick out your tongue like you are licking the ice-cream cone.

I love you

Hold up the right Y hand, with the index finger extended, and shake the arm slightly from side to side.

Memory aid: The little finger represents *I,* the index and the thumb together represent the *L* for *love,* and the thumb and the little finger together indicate the *Y* for *you.*

Tip: When you have to say good-bye to a child at school or daycare, you can wave *I love you* to them from the window or doorway. The sign is most effective when you direct it toward the person to whom you are referring.

in, enter

Slide the right Open B hand underneath the left Open B hand and come out the other side.

Memory aid: The right hand represents something going in. Think of entering a hut or a cave.

Tip: You can use this sign to say, "It's time to go in the house now."

inside, into

Place the fingertips of the right Flat O hand into the opening of the left O hand.

Memory aid: Picture putting something into a container.

Tip: You can use this sign to tell your child to put an object inside another object.

jam, jelly

Scoop the tip of the right little finger into the upturned left palm.

Memory aid: Imagine spreading jelly on a piece of bread.

Jell-O

Twist the right Bent 5 hand back and forth over the left palm.

Memory aid: The Jell-O is jiggling on the hand.

Jesus

Touch the center of the left palm with the middle finger of the right 5 hand and then reverse the motion, touching the center of the right palm with the middle finger of the left 5 hand.

Memory aid: The middle fingers are touching the scars from the crucifixion.

juice (1)

Slide the little finger of the right hand from the corner of the mouth down the chin several times.

Memory aid: Think of juice dripping down the chin.

juice (2)

Twist the right I hand back and forth in front of the body a few times.

Memory aid: The movement of the sign resembles a *J*, which represents the initial letter of *juice*.

Tip: This sign is easy for infants and toddlers to use and remember.

jump

Bounce the fingertips of the right Bent V hand on the left palm several times.

Memory aid: The fingers represent the legs of a person jumping up and down.

Tip: You can also bend and straighten the fingers. You can add more information to this sign by changing the height or quickness of the jump.

jump rope

Move both A hands in small forward circles.

Memory aid: Mime jumping rope.

Tip: You can use this sign for both the action of jumping rope and for the jump rose itself.

---

kangaroo

Bounce both 8 hands in small arches away from the body; then flick the middle fingers off the thumbs.

Memory aid: This sign is borrowed from the Australian sign for *jump* or *hop*.

---

ketchup

Hit the left O hand with the right palm several times.

Memory aid: Imagine hitting the bottom of the ketchup bottle.

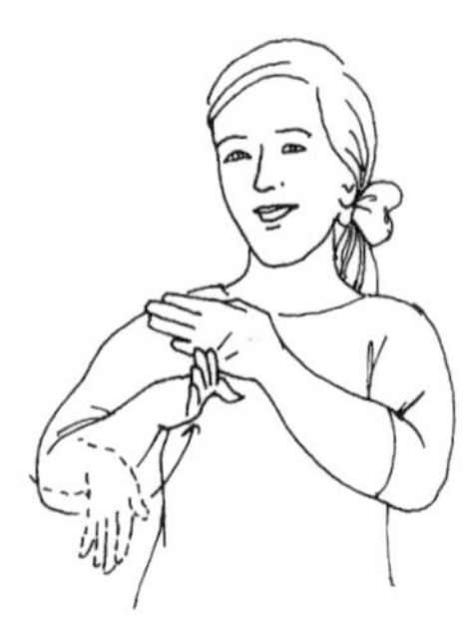

kick

Swing the right Open B hand up to hit the little finger of the left B hand.

Memory aid: The right hand represents the foot kicking an object.

Tip: The *kick* sign can be used with *no* or with a headshake when telling a child not to kick another child.

kiss

Bring Flat O hands together so fingertips tap and then separate.

Memory aid: The fingertips represent the mouths kissing.

Tip: You also can place one Flat O hand on the cheek to sign *kiss on the cheek.*

kitchen

Place the thumb of the right K hand on the left palm and then flip over the right hand.

Memory aid: Picture flipping pancakes (or eggs or hamburgers) in a pan.

kitten (baby + cat)

baby: Place the upturned right hand inside the left palm and rock hands from side to side.

cat: Place both F hands on the cheeks and pull the hands away as if stroking whiskers.

---

knife

The index finger of the right hand strokes down and across the left index finger several times.

Memory aid: The knife is sharpening a piece of wood.

---

know

Tap the fingertips of the right Bent B hand just above the eyebrow a few times.

Memory aid: Information is stored in the brain.

Tip: You can use this sign while also shaking your head for *don't know.*

lamb (baby + sheep)

baby: Place the right hand and forearm on the left hand and forearm and rock the arms side to side.

sheep: Run the back of the right V hand along the left forearm from the wrist to elbow, opening and closing the fingers of the V hand like scissors

Memory aid: The motion in the sign indicates shearing the sheep.

last, final

Bring the right little finger down and brush it past the top of the left little finger.

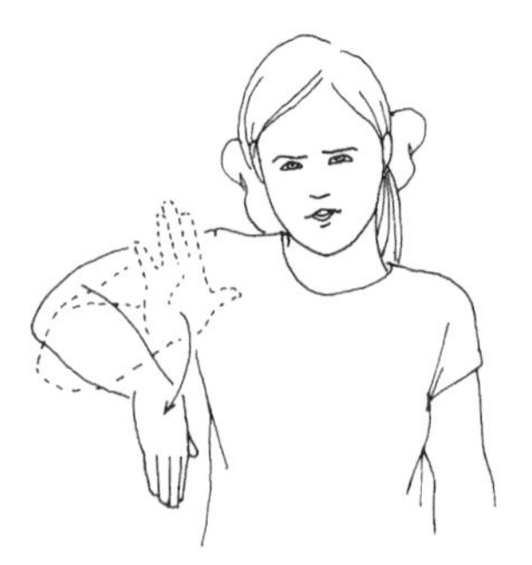

late

Hold the right 5 hand up near the shoulder then bend the arm down and swing the hand back.

Memory aid: Behind schedule.

Tip: You can use this sign with little ones when you want to say *not yet,* but you must repeat the movement.

later

Place the thumb of the right L hand in the middle of the left palm and bend the right hand down.

Memory aid: The minute hand of the clock is moving forward.

---

laugh

Put the tips of the index fingers of both L hands at the corners of the mouth and then brush the index fingers back off the face several times. Smile while you sign.

Memory aid: The fingers show the wide smile on the face.

Tip: Add some fun to the sign and laugh while signing this word.

---

left

Move the right L hand to the left.

Memory aid: The L is the initial letter of *left,* and the hand moves to the left.

lemon

Hit the back of the left B hand with the thumb of the right L hand and slide the thumb off and out several times.

Memory aid: The L hand is slicing the lemon.

lettuce, cabbage

Bump the right side of the head several times with the heel of the right 5 hand.

Memory aid: Touching the head corresponds to the head of lettuce. The fingers represent the leaves.

library

Move the right L hand in small clockwise circles.

light (illumination)

Place the thumb and middle finger of the right hand on the chin and flick the middle finger off of the thumb several times.

like (emotion)

Place the right thumb and middle finger on the chest and then move the hand away from the body while closing the thumb and middle finger.

Memory aid: Imagine the feelings coming out.

lion

Start with the fingers of the right Bent 5 hand at the hairline and draw the hand back toward the back of the head.

Memory aid: The motion outlines the mane of the lion.

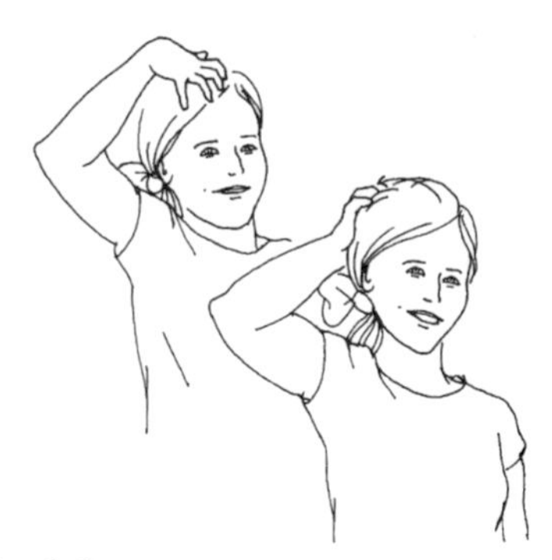

Tip: Be sure to give a big growl while signing this sign so children will associate the sound with the sign.

little

Hunch the right shoulder and move the slightly cupped hands toward each other in small quick movements.

Memory aid: The motion indicates a small size or amount.

lizard

Move the right L hand up the back of the left arm, bending and straightening the right index finger as it moves up the arm.

Memory aid: Picture the bending finger as a thin lizard moving up the arm.

lollipop, sucker

Move the right X hand in small circles toward the mouth.

Memory aid: Mime licking a lollipop.

Tip: The sign for *ice cream* is very similar, but is made with an S hand (see page 89).

long

Move the right L hand up the back of the left arm, from the wrist to the shoulder.

Memory aid: Think of long arms.

loud

Point to the right ear with the right index finger and then open to a 5 hand and shake the hand down and out several times.

Memory aid: A loud noise shakes everything around it.

love

Place the Open B hands on top of each other over the heart.

Memory aid: The heart is full of love.

Tip: A variation of this sign is made by crossing the S hands on the chest (like a hug on the heart).

low

Push the right Open B hand down about 1 or 2 inches. This sign can be repeated a few times to indicate varying degrees of lowness.

Memory aid: You push something down to make it lower.

lunch

Tap the chin several times with the thumb of the right L hand.

Tip: If you can't remember the sign for *lunch,* you can always sign *eat* instead.

macaroni

Begin with the fingertips of the M hands facing each other, then move the hands apart while raising and lowering the M fingers in a wavy motion.

Memory aid: The wavy motion represents the arched shape of the noodles, and the M hands remind you of the initial letter of *macaroni.*

mad

Move the right Bent 5 hand in toward the face.

Memory aid: Think of anger flashing in the eyes.

Tip: While signing this word, have on your mad face so your child can associate the true feeling with the sign.

---

mail, letter

Place the right thumb on the tongue and then put it on the fingertips of the left Open B hand.

Memory aid: Mimic putting a stamp on a letter.

---

man

Start with the right Flat O hand on the forehead, then bring the hand down while changing to a 5 hand, and end with the thumb on the chest.

Memory aid: The forehead is the male area of the face, and the chest position indicates the idea of sophistication; thus, a *man* is a sophisticated *boy*.

Tip: You can make an alternate version of the sign by placing the thumb of the 5 hand on the forehead and then moving down to the chest.

marbles

Start with the right F hand in front of the body, then twist the hand over while closing the hand and flick the thumb off the index finger.

Memory aid: Show the small ball and then flick the marble.

marker (color + marker)

color: Place the fingertips of the right 5 hand on the chin and wiggle the fingers.

marker: Move the right M hand in a zigzag pattern down the left palm.

Tip: *Marker* can be finger-spelled if your child can understand the spelling.

marshmallow

Squeeze and open the fingers and thumb of the Flat O hand several times as if you were squeezing a marshmallow.

Memory aid: Marshmallows are very soft.

Tip: You can also sign *white* first and then sign *marshmallow.*

McDonalds (1)

Tap the right M hand on the back of the left hand, and then tap the right D hand on the back of the left hand.

McDonalds (2)

Using both M hands, outline an M shape in front of the body starting in the center of the M.

Memory aid: Picture McDonald's golden arches.

me

Tap the chest with the right index finger.

Tip: Note that the sign for *me* is not the same as the sign for *mine*.

meat

Pinch the left hand between the thumb and index finger with the right index finger and thumb.

Memory aid: Think of the meaty part of the hand.

medicine

Move the tip of the right bent middle finger in small circles on the center of the left palm.

Memory aid: Imagine that you are crushing a pill in your hand.

Tip: Babies might use their index finger rather than the middle finger.

middle

The right bent middle finger circles once over the left palm and then lands in the center of the palm.

Memory aid: The left palm is the target, and the right finger circles and then lands in the bull's eye.

milk

Squeeze the right C hand into an S hand several times. You may use one or two hands for this sign.

Memory aid: Visualize milking a cow.

Tip: *Milk* is a great first sign. Be sure to sign it every time that you ask your baby whether he or she wants milk (with the raised eyebrow question face) or every time you give baby a bottle. This sign also can be used for *formula*.

---

mine

Pat the chest with the right Open B hand a couple of times.

Memory aid: Picture holding something close to your body to keep it from others, as a child might do.

---

mirror

Position the Open B hand in front of the face and twist the hand several times.

Memory aid: Picture looking into a mirror to see your reflection.

mittens

Slip imaginary mittens over each hand.

Mohammed, Islam, Muslim

Position both upright Open B hands above the shoulders then bend the arms down while bowing the head.

Memory aid: Think of bowing in respect.

monkey

With elbows out and using both Bent 5 hands, scratch upward on each side of the chest.

Memory aid: Think about how a monkey behaves.

Tip: Be sure to show a monkey face and make the monkey noises along with this sign.

moon

Place the right Modified C hand on the temple and move it out and up toward the sky.

Memory aid: Envision a crescent moon.

---

more

Tap the fingertips of both Flat O hands together several times.

Memory aid: Add one to another.

Tip: More should be one of the first signs you teach your child. You can use it during mealtime, bath time, playtime, story time, and basically anytime during the day. Children may sign this crudely at first, but if you keep signing it correctly, they will too. Remember to use the appropriate facial expression if you are asking whether your child wants more.

---

morning

Place the left hand in the crook of the right arm and raise the right forearm slowly.

Memory aid: The left arm represents the horizon. The right hand is the sun rising over the horizon.

Moses

Tap the fingertips of the upright left hand with the index finger of the right M hand and then move the right hand down to tap the center of the left palm.

mother, mommy

Tap the chin several times with the thumb of the right 5 hand.

Memory aid: The sign is made on the female part of the face.

Tip: The sign also can be made by placing the thumb of the right 5 hand on the chin and wiggling the fingers.

motorcycle

Twist both S hands outward at the wrist several times, as though revving the engine of a motorcycle.

Tip: Add some fun by using a motorcycle sound while signing this word.

mouse

Brush the tip of the nose with the right index finger a couple of times.

Memory aid: A mouse twitches its nose.

---

movie

Place the heel of the right 5 hand on the left palm and slide the right hand from side to side.

Memory aid: Think of the frames of the film moving through the projector.

---

music, song

Swing the right B hand back and forth in small motions inside the left forearm.

Memory aid: Picture the movement of the conductor's hand.

Tip: The sign for *sing* is different (see page 144).

nap

Rest the left cheek gently on the back of the right Open B hand.

Tip: You also can use this sign for *bed* or *night, night.*

napkin

Brush the fingertips of the right A hand across the mouth a couple of times.

Memory aid: The right hand represents a napkin wiping off the mouth.

need, necessary

Bounce the right X hand downward two times.

Memory aid: Visualize hooking something you need and pinning it down.

Tip: You can use this sign to mean *must* or *have to* if you move the hand down once.

nice

Slide the right Open B hand off the left Open B palm several times.

Memory aid: Think of a nice, fresh clean surface.

Tip: You can use this sign to tell children to be nice to one another.

---

night

Slowly move the right Bent B hand down on the back of the left wrist.

Memory aid: Imagine the sun moving down below the horizon.

---

no

Open and close the right index and middle fingers down on the thumb a few times.

Memory aid: Think of spelling *no*.

nose

Touch the tip of the nose with the right index finger.

now

Place both Y hands in front of the chest and drop them down slightly.

Memory aid: Something is placed in the hands at this instant.

Tip: You can use this sign to tell a child, "Come here now."

number

Tap the fingertips of the right Flat O hand on the fingertips of the left Flat O hand, and then reverse the hand positions.

nurse (medical)

Tap the index and middle fingers of the right N hand on the inside of the left wrist.

Memory aid: The *n* is the initial letter of *nurse,* and the nurse is taking a pulse.

---

ocean

Tap the index finger of the right W hand on the chin. Then move both Open B hands away from the body in a wavy motion.

Memory aid: Picture the waves on the water.

octopus

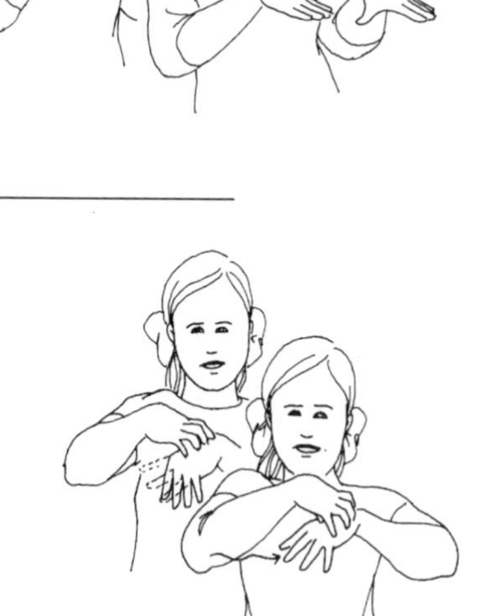

Place the fingers of the right hand on the back of the left hand, and then move both hands to the left while wiggling the fingers of the left hand.

Memory aid: The left-hand fingers represent the legs of the octopus, and the right hand is the animal's head.

off

Place the right Open B hand on the back of the left Open B hand, then lift the right hand off of the left hand.

okay

Fingerspell *o-k*.

old

Close the right S hand just below the chin and move it down in a wavy motion.

Memory aid: Visualize an old man's wavy beard.

on

Place the right Open B hand on the back of the left Open B hand.

open the door

Place the B hands side-by-side in front of the chest, and then twist the right hand back.

orange (color, fruit)

Open and close the right S hand at the tip of the chin.

Memory aid: Squeeze the juice from an orange into your mouth.

out

Pull the right O hand out of the curved opening of the left C hand.

Memory aid: Picture taking something out of a container.

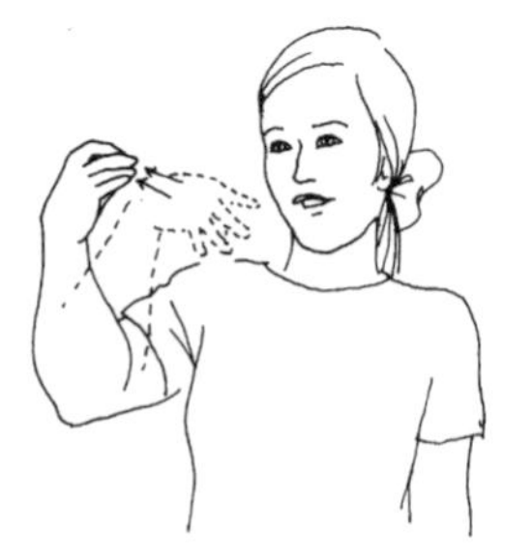

outside

Position the right 5 hand at shoulder level and then move it away from the body while closing to a Flat O hand.

Memory aid: Think of moving your body from inside to outside.

over

Slide the right Open B hand across the back of the left hand.

Memory aid: Picture putting a blanket over a bed.

owl

Place O hands over the eyes and bend the hands down and up twice.

Memory aid: The hands represent the owl's large eyes.

Tip: Make the owl's hooting sound while signing this word.

---

pacifier

Move the modified right C hand toward the mouth several times.

Memory aid: Think of inserting a pacifier into the mouth.

---

pain

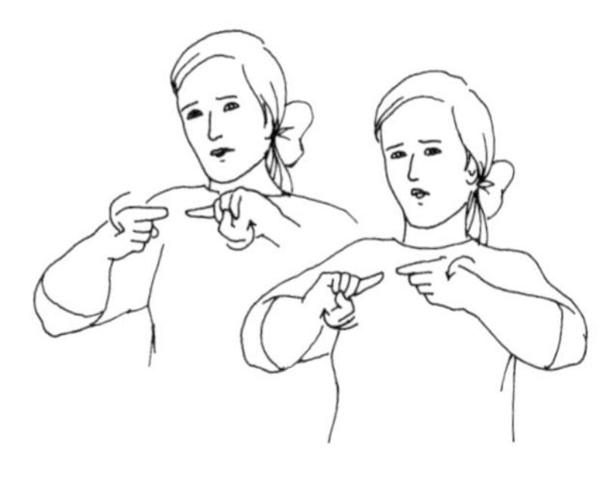

Twist the 1 hands in opposite directions in front of the body.

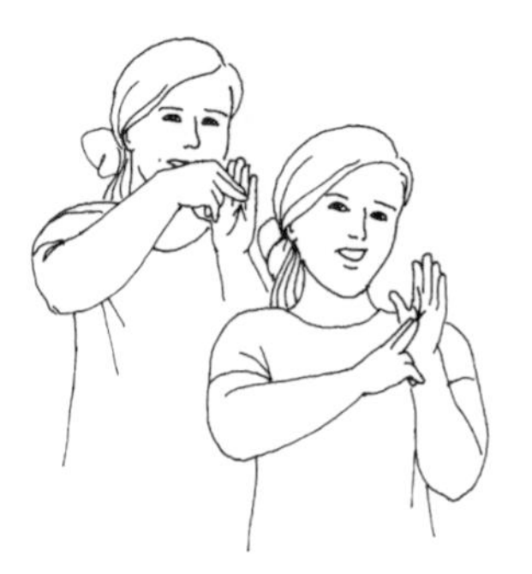

paint

Gently stroke the index and middle fingers of the right hand up and down the upturned left palm.

Memory aid: The fingers represent the brush, and the palm represents the canvas.

pajamas

Place the index fingers of both P hands on the chest and then flip the hands over.

Memory aid: The *p* is the initial letter of *pajamas.*

pancake

Flip the right Open B hand over and back on the left palm several times.

Memory aid: Picture flipping over a pancake.

paper

Smack the heels of both palms together and then slide the hands off each other.

Memory aid: Imagine the pulp being pressed.

---

party

Swing the wrists of both P hands left to right in front of the body.

Memory aid: The movement of the hands represents the people moving around at a party.

peas

Bounce the middle finger of the right P hand in small arches along the left index finger.

Memory aid: Think of peas in a pod.

peacock

Place the right A hand on the back of the left wrist and then open the fingers of the right hand in a fanning motion.

Memory aid: The fanned hand represents the peacock's tail.

peanut butter (peanut + butter)

peanut: Flick the thumbnail of the right A hand off the front teeth.

butter: Slide the fingers of the right H hand off the heel of the left palm.

Memory aid: In the sign for *peanut,* the teeth break the nutshell. In the sign for *butter,* picture spreading butter on bread.

penguin

Move the shoulders alternately up and down, with the arms down to the sides and the hands extended.

Memory aid: Imitate the way a penguin moves its body.

person

Place the P hands near the shoulders and move them straight down.

---

pet (noun, verb)

Rub the back of the left Open B hand with the fingers of the right Open B hand.

Memory aid: Imagine petting an animal gently.

Tip: Use this sign to tell a child to be gentle or nice to another child or animal.

---

pie

Make two diagonal slices on the left palm using the side of the right Open B hand.

Memory aid: Imitate slicing a pie into pieces.

pig

Place the back of the right hand under the chin and bend the fingers down and up several times.

Memory aid: Imagine the pig's snout dipping into the trough as it eats.

Tip: Make a snorting sound with this sign or say "oink, oink" so the child associates the animal sound with the sign.

pillow

Rest the right thumb on the cheek and bring the fingertips toward the face several times.

Memory aid: Squeeze an imaginary soft pillow.

pizza

Touch the chin with the index finger of the right modified C hand, then bring both modified C hands down and swing them out slightly two times.

Memory aid: Picture the outline of a round pizza.

Tip: You also can sign just the first half of this sign.

plate

Hold out both modified C hands to show the size of a plate.

Tip: If the plate is small, hold hands closer together. If the plate is large, hold hands farther apart.

play

Shake both Y hands from side to side.

Tip: This sign also can be made using one hand.

please

Move the right Open B hand in small circles on the chest.

Memory aid: Think about someone pleading.

Tip: Small babies can learn to sign *please,* and when they do, they will be so cute that you will want to give them anything!

police officer

Rest the modified right C hand on the chest, below the left shoulder.

Memory aid: The position at the shoulder signifies a place of authority. The C handshape stands for care because the police *care* about people.

pony (horse + short)

horse: Place the thumb of the right H hand on the right temple and bend the extended fingers down a few times

short: Push the Open B hand down in front of the body.

Memory aid: Think of a small horse.

popcorn

Alternately raise each hand while flicking up the index finger from the thumb.

Memory aid: Visualize the corn kernels popping.

porcupine

Rest the right S hand on the back of the left S hand, then open the right hand.

Memory aid: Picture the porcupine's quills sticking up.

---

potato

Tap the fingertips of the right Bent V hand on the back of the left hand.

Memory aid: The fork pokes holes in the potato.

---

potato chips

potato: Tap the fingertips of the right Bent V hand on the back of the left hand.

chip: Draw a circle with the index fingers of both hands.

pregnant

Bring the 5 hands together and interlock the fingers in front of the stomach.

Memory aid: Show the roundness of the stomach.

present, gift

Start with both X hands upright and then bend them down in a small arch.

Memory aid: Act out giving a gift.

pretzel

Start with the tips of the index fingers touching and then twist the hands out and around until the fingers cross.

Memory aid: Picture the shape of a pretzel.

pudding

Scoop the middle finger of the right P hand out of the palm of the left hand and bring the right hand to the mouth. Repeat the movement.

Memory aid: Scoop the pudding out of a bowl and bring the spoon up to the mouth.

---

pull

Using both A hands, pull an imaginary rope toward the body.

---

pumpkin

Place the right 8 hand on the back of the left hand and snap the middle finger off the right thumb. Then show the size of the pumpkin with C hands facing each other.

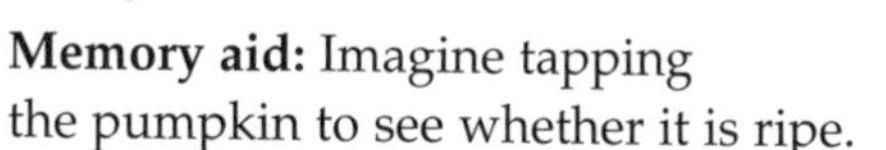

Memory aid: Imagine tapping the pumpkin to see whether it is ripe.

Tip: *Pumpkin* also can be signed with only the first part of the sign.

punish, discipline

Brush the right index finger off the left elbow with a quick downward motion.

puppy (baby + dog)

baby: Place the upturned right hand inside the left palm and rock hands from side to side.

dog: Pat the thigh a few times.

Tip: You also can just sign *dog*.

push

Push both Open B hands away from the body.

Memory aid: Think of a pushing motion.

Tip: Sign *no push* to let a child know that it is not okay to push another child.

puzzle

Starting at the chin, move both A hands down in alternating jagged motions.

Memory aid: Show the curved lines of a puzzle.

---

quiet

Cross both Open B hands at the chin and bring them down and apart until both hands are facing down.

Memory aid: Envision pushing down the noise.

Tip: This sign is a much better way to tell a child to be quiet than saying "shhh" with the finger in front of the mouth because this sign suggests that not only noise but also movement (including signing hands) should stop.

---

rabbit, bunny

Place both H hands on the temples and bend the H fingers down a few times.

Memory aid: Picture the rabbit's ears moving back and forth.

raccoon

Place the V hands over the eyes and then move the hands out toward the ears.

Memory aid: Picture the mask of a raccoon's face.

Tip: Note how this sign differs slightly from the sign for *Halloween.*

rain

Start with both Bent 5 hands at shoulder height and move the hands down in short, quick movements.

Memory aid: Show raindrops falling from the sky.

raisin

Bounce the index and middle fingers of the right R hand down the back of the left hand.

Memory aid: Show grapes on a vine using a R hand to represent *raisins.*

read

Brush the right V hand fingers down the upturned left palm.

Memory aid: The right V fingers represent the eyes, and the left palm is the page. The eyes scan down the page.

---

ready

Cross the R hands in front of the body and swing the hands away from each other.

Memory aid: Think of lining up things in order.

---

red

Rub the right index finger down the bottom lip and slide it off the chin.

Memory aid: Think of red lips or lipstick.

refrigerator

Begin with the S hands at shoulder level and shake them in a shivering motion. Then bring the A hands together and pull them apart. and twist the right hand back.

Memory aid: Sign *cold* and then open the refrigerator door.

reindeer

Place the thumbs of both 5 hands on the temples and then bring the hands down, closing them A hands.

Tug both hands down in small movements.

Memory aid: At first, the hands are the antlers of the reindeer; then they close to hold the reins of a sleigh.

right (correct)

Bring the right 1 hand down on top of the left 1 hand.

Memory aid: Think of the phrase "right on the dot." The left hand is the dot.

right (direction)

Move the right R hand from the left to the right.

Memory aid: Move the hand to the right with an R to symbolize the direction.

---

room, box

Place the right Open B hand in back of the left Open B hand and swing the hands out so the palms are facing each other.

Memory aid: Show the four walls of the room or of a box.

Tip: Adjust the distance between the hands to show the size of the box or room. Some signers use R hands when signing *room.*

---

rooster

Rest the thumb of the right 3 hand on the middle of the forehead.

Memory aid: Envision a rooster's comb.

run

Wrap the index finger of the right L hand around the thumb of the left L hand and wiggle the thumbs and index fingers as the hands move forward in a quick motion.

Memory aid: Picture two runners passing the baton during a relay race.

sad

Cross the right 5 hand over the left 5 hand in front of the face; then move both hands down to the chest, using a sad facial expression.

Memory aid: The sadness comes from the eyes to the heart.

Tip: You can also use the one-hand version of *cry* to mean *sad* (see p. 50).

safe

Cross the S hands at the wrist in front of the body, and then swing the hands apart.

same, like, similar

Bring the 1 hands together in front of the body so the index fingers touch.

Memory aid: Picture holding two things side by side to show that they are the same.

Tip: Bounce the index fingers together to mean *similar.*

---

sandwich

Place the right Bent B hand over the left Bent B hand and bring both hands toward the mouth.

Memory aid: Picture putting two pieces of bread together and eating them.

Santa Claus

Start with the Bent 5 hands at each cheek, and then arc the hands out and down twice toward the chest.

Memory aid: Show Santa's big, full beard.

scared

Position the S hands on either side of the chest, then move the hands toward each other quickly while opening them into 5 hands.

Memory aid: The heart is in fear.

Tip: Use a surprised facial expression to show your child the true meaning of the word.

school

Strike the heels of the palms against each other two times.

Memory aid: The teacher claps for attention.

scissors

Open and close the extended fingers of the right V hand several times.

Memory aid: The fingers mimic the action of scissors.

screwdriver

Twist the tips of the extended fingers of the right H hand back and forth into the palm of the left Open B hand.

Memory aid: Show the motion of using a screwdriver.

---

seal

Open and close the Open B hands at the heels of the palms several times.

Memory aid: Visualize the seal's flippers clapping together.

Tip: Be sure to make the barking seal noise along with the sign.

---

search

Move the right C hand in small circles in front of the face.

Memory aid: The eyes keep searching and searching.

shampoo

Shake both Bent 5 hands back and forth on the sides of the head.

Memory aid: Mimic washing the hair.

Tip: You also can use this sign to mean "wash your hair."

share

Swing the right Open B hand back and forth along the index finger of the left hand.

Memory aid: Think of "a little for me, a little for you."

Tip: *Share* is a great sign to use at home and in preschool. Children may learn the sign before they understand the concept of sharing.

shark

Sit the B hand on top of the head.

Memory aid: The hand represents the shark's fin.

shave

Rub the thumb of the right Y hand down the left cheek and then down the right cheek.

Memory aid: Picture a man shaving his face.

---

sheep

Open and close the fingers of the right V hand along the left forearm, starting at the wrist.

Memory aid: Think of shearing a sheep's wool.

Tip: Make the sheep sound while signing.

---

shirt

Pinch a bit of material in front of the right shoulder with the right index finger and thumb.

Memory aid: Show where the shirt is located.

shoes

Tap the S hands together two times.

Memory aid: Remember Dorothy clicking the heels of her ruby slippers in *The Wizard of Oz.*

Tip: Hide the child's shoes behind your back and sign *where shoes?* Remember to use the appropriate questioning facial expression.

short

Place the right Bent B hand in front of the body and push the hand down a few times.

shower

Position the right Flat O hand above the head and open and close the hand several times.

Memory aid: Show the water coming out of the showerhead.

shy

Place the bent right fingers, with the thumb down, on the cheek and gently twist the hand forward.

Memory aid: The color rises in the cheeks of a blushing shy person.

---

sick

Place the middle finger of the right 5 hand on the forehead and the middle finger of the left 5 hand on the stomach.

Memory aid: Your head and stomach hurt.

Tip: Your facial expression should show that you don't feel well.

---

sign language (sign + language)

sign: Point the index fingers at each other and move them in alternating circles toward the body.

language: Begin with the thumbs of both L hands touching; then move the hands apart with a slight wavy motion.

Memory aid: *Sign* shows the constant motion of the hands while signing. *Language* is made with *L*s that move with the sound waves.

silly

Brush the thumb of the right Y hand off the tip of the nose a few times.

Memory aid: Picture a playful clown. The Y hand represents playing, and the nose represents the clown's nose.

sing

Touch the mouth with the extended fingers of the right H hand and move the hand in small circles away from the mouth. You may use one hand or two hands.

Memory aid: The two fingers represent singing in harmony.

Tip: Note that this sign is different from the sign for *song*. See *song*.

sister

Place the thumb of the right L hand on the chin and bring the hand down to rest on top of the left L hand.

Memory aid: The L hand is placed at the chin, which is the female part of the face.

sit

Move the bent fingers of the right V hand down to sit on the extended fingers of the left H hand.

Memory aid: The bent fingers represent the legs sitting on a chair.

Tip: You can sign *sit* from across the room when a child can't hear you, which is both convenient and safe.

---

skate, ice skate, roller skate (noun, verb)

skate (verb): Swing both X hands (for *ice skate*) or both Bent V hands (for *roller skate*), from left to right.

skates (noun): Hold both X hands (for *ice skates*) or both Bent V hands (for *roller skates*), out in front of the body.

Memory aid: The X hands in the sign *ice skate* represent the single blade of the skate. The Bent V hands for the sign *roller skate* show the wheels of the skate.

---

sleep, sleepy

Start with the right 4 hand in front of the face, and then bring the hand down slightly and close it while closing the eyes.

Memory aid: The eyes are falling asleep.

Tip: When asking whether a child is getting sleepy, remember to use a questioning facial expression.

slipper

Slide the right C hand under the left Open B hand.

Memory aid: Picture sliding the slipper onto the foot.

slow

Place the fingertips of the right Open B hand on the fingernails of the left hand and slowly slide the right hand along the back of the left hand.

Memory aid: Think of a snail slowly moving from one place to another.

small, little, tiny

Push the Open B hands toward each other to show how small an object is. The hands also can move toward each other in small movements.

Tip: If the object is very small, you can use the thumb and index finger of the right hand (instead of both hands) to show the size.

smart, clever

Put the index finger of the right 1 hand on the forehead and bend the hand forward.

Memory aid: Imagine smart brain waves traveling out of the head.

---

smell

Bring the right Open B hand up from the mouth to the nose, and then brush it off the nose in small, repeated movements.

Memory aid: The air is going into the nose.

---

snake

Position the back of the right Bent V hand in front of the mouth, and move the hand away from the body in a zigzag pattern.

Memory aid: The fingers are the snake's fangs, and the zigzag motion is the snake slithering in the grass.

Tip: Make the snake's hissing sound while signing.

snow

Wiggle the fingers of both 5 hands as they float slowly down.

Memory aid: Picture the snowflakes drifting down.

Tip: *Rain* is signed differently. See *rain.*

soap

Brush the fingertips of the right Bent B hand off the palm and heel of the left hand.

Memory aid: Think of carving the soap.

soccer

Swing the right Open B hand up to hit the little finger of the left hand two times.

Memory aid: Think of kicking a soccer ball.

Tip: This sign is the same as *kick,* except for the repeated movement.

socks

Rub the sides of the index fingers together.

Memory aid: Envision knitting the socks.

soda, coke, pop

Place the thumb and index finger of the right F hand into the center of the left S hand; lift up the right hand, open it, and bring it down on top of the left hand.

Memory aid: Imagine putting a cork into a bottle and then hitting it to make sure it is secure.

soft

Start with both 5 hands up near the shoulders, then bring the hands down slightly while gently opening and closing the Flat O hands.

Memory aid: The motion of the sign shows squeezing something soft.

sore throat

Rub the throat gently up and down with the right C hand.

Memory aid: It hurts to touch the throat.

Tip: Your face should have a painful expression. Note that *sore throat* does not involve the actual *hurt* sign, but if you sign *hurt* in front of the throat, the meaning will be clear.

sorry

Move the right S hand in small circles on the chest.

Memory aid: The *S* is the initial letter of *sorry,* and it moves over the heart to show that the heart is sorrowful.

Tip: Show a very sad facial expression to help the child understand the meaning of the word. Children are able to make and use this sign at an early age.

sour, pickle

Dig the index finger sharply into the chin and twist it from side to side.

Tip: Use your sour facial expression. The same sign can be used for *pickle.*

spaghetti

Begin with the tips of the little fingers of both I hands touching, and then move the hands apart in a wavy motion.

Memory aid: Show the shape of a long, wavy noodle.

---

spider

Rest the right Bent 5 hand on top of the left Bent 5 hand, then wiggle all the fingers as the hands crawl to the right.

Memory aid: The fingers represent the wiggling legs of the spider as it moves.

---

spoon, soup

Place the extended fingers of the right H hand on the extended fingers of the left H hand and raise the right hand up to the mouth.

Memory aid: The left fingers represent the bowl, and the right fingers represent the spoon. You are scooping food out of a bowl and placing it into the mouth.

square

Trace the outline of a square with both index fingers, starting at the center top of the square.

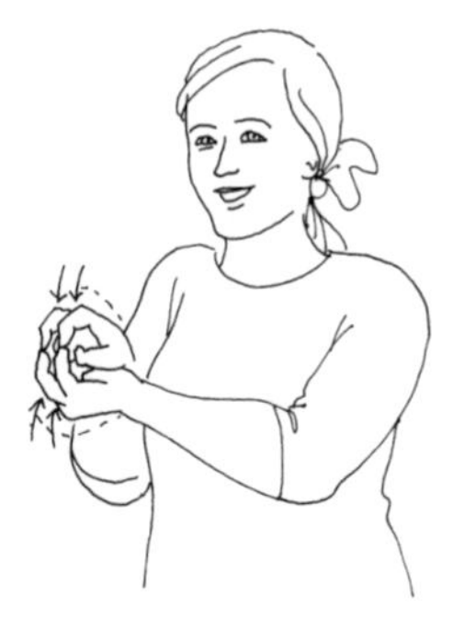

squirrel

Tap the fingertips of both Bent V hands together.

Memory aid: Picture the squirrel's teeth breaking a nut.

Tip: Make the squirrel's chattering sound while making the sign.

stamp (postal)

Touch the lips with the extended fingertips of the right H hand, bring the hand down, and rest it on the extended fingers of the left H hand.

Memory aid: Think about licking a stamp and placing it on a letter.

stamp (rubber)

Bounce the side of the right S hand on the left palm.

stand

Position the extended fingers of the upside-down V hand on the left palm.

Memory aid: The fingers represent the legs standing.

start

Insert the index finger of the right 1 hand between the index finger and middle finger of the left hand, and then twist the right index finger forward.

Memory aid: Think of starting a car by turning the key in the ignition.

stay (1)

Bring the right Y hand down in an emphatic motion.

Memory aid: Imagine keeping someone in his or her seat.

stay (2)

Begin with the thumbs of the Y hands touching, then arc the right hand forward and down.

stink

Wave the right Open B hand up and down in front of the nose.

Memory aid: Imagine reacting to a bad smell.

Tip: Be sure to use an appropriate facial expression (for example, a crinkled nose).

stomach ache, tummy ache

Rub the stomach with the right 5 hand while making a pained facial expression.

Memory aid: Rub a sore tummy.

stop

Sharply hit the left palm with the side of the right Open B hand.

Memory aid: Stop an action.

Tip: Be sure to look stern while signing *stop*. The child needs to know that you are serious.

store

Begin with the wrists of both Flat O hands bent down, and then bend the wrists up and down twice.

Memory aid: Think of pushing a shopping cart.

story

Move the hands in a circular motion toward each other, link the thumbs and index fingers as they come together, and continue the circle back to the original position. Repeat this movement a few times.

Memory aid: Envision bringing a bunch of words together to make a story.

Tip: It is easier for little ones to sign *book* rather than *story*. You can use the sign for *book* (with a questioning facial expression) when asking whether the child wants to read a story.

stove, oven

Slide the right Open B hand underneath the left Open B hand.

Memory aid: Think of placing a dish into the oven.

strawberry

Gently slide the index finger and thumb of the right F hand from the mouth to the chin a couple of times.

Memory aid: Picture pulling the stem off of a strawberry with the mouth.

strong

Flex both biceps and shake both S hands in a short, quick, motion

Memory aid: Furrow the eyebrows and make a stern face with this sign.

---

summer

Brush the index finger of the right 1 hand across the forehead and end by bending the index finger.

Memory aid: Think of wiping sweat from the brow.

---

sun

Tap the temple with the right C hand a couple of times.

Memory aid: The sunlight shines in your eyes.

swan

Rest the elbow of the right arm, with a Flat O hand, on the back of the left hand.

Memory aid: The arm is the long neck of the swan and the Flat O hand is the beak.

sweater

Place the fingertips of the Bent B hands near the shoulders and run them down the body to the waist.

Memory aid: The sign shows the location of the sweater.

sweep

Brush the side of the right Open B hand off the palm and fingers of the left hand.

Memory aid: Picture brushing the dirt off the floor or ground.

sweet, sugar

Brush the fingertips of the right Open B hand off the chin while bending the fingers and repeat two times.

Memory aid: Think of a sweet taste on the lips.

Tip: The sign also can be used to call someone sweet or to ask (with the appropriate question facial expression) whether something tastes sweet.

---

swim

Position both Bent B hands in front of the chest and move them away from the body in small circular motions.

Memory aid: Picture swimming the breaststroke, pushing the water to the side as you swim.

---

swimming pool (swim + pool)

swim: Position both Bent B hands in front of the chest and move them away from the body in small circular motions.

pool: Hold the Modified C hands apart to show the shape of the pool.

swing

Rest the fingers of the right H hand on the back of the fingers of the left H hand and swing both hands back and forth a few times.

table

Tap the right forearm and hand on the back of the left forearm and hand.

Memory aid: Picture a hard, flat surface.

tall (height)

Raise the right Bent B hand from shoulder level to above the head.

Tip: Use this sign to show how tall a person is or how much he or she has grown.

tall (object)

Slide the right index finger straight up the left palm.

Memory aid: The sign shows the height of an object.

---

tape (noun, verb)

Slide the extended fingers of the right H hand across the back of the left hand.

Memory aid: Think of sticking a piece of tape to an object.

---

teacher

Place both Flat O hands, fingers facing forward, at the temples and move the hands straight out from the forehead. Then, change into B hands and move the hands straight down the sides of the body.

Memory aid: Knowledge comes from the mind. The hands move down to represent a person.

Tip: If you sign just the first part of *teacher* and push the hands forward in two small movements, the sign becomes *teach*.

teddy bear (doll + bear)

doll: Brush the right X finger down the nose two times.

bear: Cross the arms on the chest and lightly scratch the chest with the fingers of both Bent 5 hands.

Memory aid: A teddy bear is a bear that is a doll.

---

teeth

Tap a side tooth with the index finger of the right X hand.

telephone, call

Place the right Y hand on the cheek with the thumb at the ear and the little finger at the mouth.

Memory aid: The hand represents the phone at the ear.

Tip: To make the verb form, as in *call* someone or *make a phone call,* sign *telephone* and then move the hand away from the face.

television, TV

Fingerspell *T-V*.

---

thank you

Start with the right Open B hand in front of the mouth and move the hand straight out. Nod and smile while you sign.

Memory aid: Picture blowing kisses to say thank you. Some toddlers will actually blow kisses to say thank you.

Tip: Be sure to sign *thank you* every time you want your little one to say thank you. He or she will start signing it at a young age.

Thanksgiving

Swing the G hand down from the chin to the chest.

Memory aid: Envision the turkey's wattle shaking.

thirsty

Run the tip of the right index finger from the chin to the throat.

Memory aid: Think of liquid running down the throat.

throw

Move the S hand straight out in a throwing motion from the shoulder, while changing to a 5 hand.

Memory aid: Picture throwing an object.

tickle

Wiggle the fingers of both Bent 5 hands.

Memory aid: Show a tickling motion in the air.

tiger

Place the fingertips of both Bent 5 hands on the cheeks, and then scrape the fingers off the cheeks.

Memory aid: Think of the tiger's stripes.

Tip: Be sure to make a growling sound while signing.

---

time

Tap the tip of the right bent index finger against the back of the left wrist several times.

Memory aid: Think of tapping a watch to check the time.

---

tired, exhausted

Rest the fingertips of both Bent B hands below the shoulders and then let both fall forward onto the chest.

Memory aid: The sign represent a deep sigh to show how tired you are.

Tip: Use a very tired facial expression.

toast

Tap the left palm with the Bent V fingers of the right hand, and then tap the back of the left hand with the Bent V fingers.

Memory aid: The bread is toasted on both sides.

together

Bring the A hands together and then move the hands forward slightly.

Memory aid: Visualize two coming together as one and acting in unison.

toilet, potty

Shake the right T hand from side to side.

Memory aid: The *t* is the initial letter of *toilet.*

Tip: Sign *toilet* every time you change your baby's diapers. For toddlers who are beginning potty training and older children who may need to be reminded, you can sign *toilet* from across the room and they will know what you mean. They also will be able to sign to you that they have to go potty. Some classroom teachers are using this sign in the classroom so children don't have to be embarrassed to ask to use the restroom.

tomato

Move the right index finger down from the mouth and brush it off the tip of the left index finger.

Memory aid: The mouth is red like the tomato, and the finger shows the slicing of the tomato.

---

tomorrow

Place the thumb of the right A hand on the right cheek and twist the hand forward.

Memory aid: The sign indicates going into the future.

---

tonight (now + night)

now: Place both Y hands in front of the chest and drop them down slightly.

night: Slowly move the right Bent B hand down on the back of the left wrist.

Memory aid: The sun is going down under the horizon now.

tools

Bounce the right T hand in small arches from the center of the body to the right side of the body.

Tip: This sign refers to all tools in general. Specific tools have their own signs (for example, see *hammer* and *screwdriver*).

toothbrush

Shake the right index finger up and down in front of the mouth. Open the mouth to show the teeth while signing.

Memory aid: Mime brushing teeth.

touch

Gently tap the back of the left hand with the middle finger of the right 5 hand.

Memory aid: Think of touching an object.

Tip: Sign *no touch* when you want a child to stay away from something.

towel

Move both S hands from left to right just above the shoulders.

Memory aid: Envision drying your back with a towel.

---

toys

Twist both T hands forward and back several times.

Memory aid: This sign is similar to the sign for *play* but you use the T hands to represent toys.

---

train

Rub the extended fingers of the right H hand back and forth along the back of the extended fingers of the left H hand.

Memory aid: Think of a train moving on the track.

Tip: Make the choo-choo sound when you sign *train* so the child will associate the sound with the sign.

tree

Rest the right elbow on the back of the left hand and twist the right 5 hand from back to front several times.

Memory aid: The right arm represents the trunk, and the fingers are the branches of the tree.

triangle

Outline the shape of a triangle with both index fingers, starting at the upper point of the triangle.

tricycle

Move the T hands alternately in small forward circles.

Memory aid: Think of the pedals of a bicycle. The T hands represent the initial letter of *tricycle.*

Tip: This sign is similar to the sign for *bicycle*, but *tricycle* uses T hands.

truck

Place the right T hand in back of the left T hand, and then pull the hands apart two times.

Memory aid: The hands show the length of the vehicle, and the T handshapes will help you remember the *T* in *truck.*

---

try

Hold both T hands down and then swing them up in an arc.

Memory aid: Think of pushing through a difficult event.

---

turkey

Place the right G hand in front of the chin, with the thumb pointing down, and shake the hand slightly.

Memory aid: Show the turkey's wattle at the neck.

turtle

Cover the right A hand with the left hand and bend the right thumb up and down twice.

Memory aid: The thumb is the turtle's head, and the left hand represents the shell.

Tip: Children enjoy making this sign.

---

twins

Slide the right T hand from the right cheek across to the left cheek.

umbrella

Put the right S hand on top of the left S hand and raise the right hand straight up.

Memory aid: Picture opening an umbrella.

uncle

Gently tap the extended fingers of the right U hand on the right temple.

Memory aid: Signs for males are made on the upper part of the face. The *U* is the initial letter of *uncle*.

---

under

Slide the right Open B hand underneath the left hand.

Memory aid: Think of moving under something.

---

understand

Position the right S hand at the right side of the forehead, and then quickly snap the index finger up.

Memory aid: Think of a light bulb going on in your brain.

underwear

Raise the F hands from the top of each leg to the waist.

Memory aid: Mimic pulling on underwear.

up

Point up to the sky with the right index finger.

vegetable

Touch the cheek with the index finger of the right V hand, then flip the hand over so the middle finger of the V hand touches the cheek.

Memory aid: Vegetables are good for the teeth.

waffle

Bounce the right W hand on the left palm twice.

Memory aid: Picture the waffle maker making imprints on the waffle.

---

wagon

Pull the right S hand from the right to the left.

Memory aid: Visualize pulling a wagon with one hand.

---

wait

Extend both 5 hands in front of the body, with the right hand out a little farther than the left hand, and wiggle all of the fingers.

Memory aid: The fingers are waiting impatiently.

walk

Swing the Open B hands alternately up and down.

Memory aid: The hands represent the feet walking.

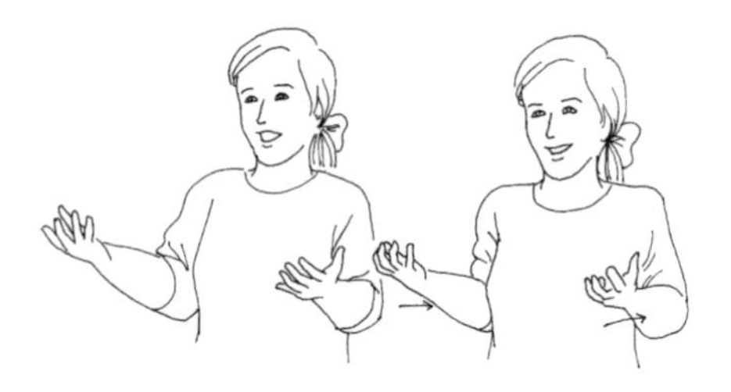

want

Extend both Bent 5 hands in front of the body, then pull the hands toward the body while bending the fingers.

Memory aid: Envision a child saying, "Give me! Give me! Give me!" while pulling the desired object in toward the body.

warm

Place the fingertips of the right O hand at the mouth, and then slowly move the hand away from the mouth while opening the fingers.

Memory aid: Show warm breath moving out of the mouth.

wash (general)

Move the S hands in alternating circles toward each other.

Memory aid: Picture washing the windows.

wash (dishes)

Rub the right A hand in small circles against the left palm.

Memory aid: Imagine scrubbing a dish with a sponge.

wash (face)

Gently move the A hands in small circles on the cheeks.

Memory aid: Picture washing the face.

water

Tap the index finger of the right W hand against the chin several times.

Memory aid: Think of drinking water.

welcome, invite, you're welcome

With a sweeping motion, glide the right Bent B hand from in front of the body toward the stomach.

Memory aid: Imagine signaling someone to come in to your home.

Tip: This sign can also be used to mean *you're welcome,* without signing *you're.*

wet

Hold up the 5 hands in front of the body, then quickly move them down while bringing the fingertips and thumbs together. The sign can be repeated.

Memory aid: Think about something being wet to the touch.

whale

Dip the right W hand in up-and-down, wavy motions along the left arm.

Memory aid: The left arm represents the ocean, and the right hand is the whale moving in and out of the water.

Tip: This sign also can be made using a Y hand to represent the whale's tail.

---

what

Scrape the index finger of the right 1 hand across the left palm.

Memory aid: What finger will you choose?

Tip: Remember to use the appropriate question facial expression when using this sign in a question.

---

wheelchair

Point the index fingers of both 1 hands toward each other on either side of the body, and move the hands in small forward circles.

Memory aid: Picture the wheels of the wheelchair moving forward.

when

Circle the tip of the left index finger with the right index finger, ending with the fingers touching.

Memory aid: When will the finger land?

Tip: Remember to use the appropriate question facial expression when using this sign in a question.

where

Shake the right 1 hand from side to side in front of the body.

Memory aid: Where is it? Is it here or over there?

Tip: This sign looks like the gesture often used for *no, no*. Try to remember that the finger is looking for something. Use this sign to play a searching game, using words that you can sign. Where are your shoes (*where shoes*)? Where is mommy (*where mommy*)? Where is your nose (*where nose*)? You can add many other items to your search, which will help you and your child practice a variety of signs. Remember to use the appropriate question facial expression.

white

Place the fingertips of the right 5 hand on the chest and then move the hand out while closing to a Flat O hand.

Memory aid: Think of a clean, white shirt.

who

Put the thumb of the right L hand on the chin; bend the index finger up and down a few times.

Tip: Purse your lips while you make this sign. If you are signing the word without using your voice, the mouth formation looks like the spoken word *who.* Remember to use the appropriate question facial expression when using this sign in a question.

---

why

Position the right Y hand, with the index finger extended, on the right side of the forehead, and then raise and lower the middle and ring fingers a few times.

Memory aid: The brain is working to understand.

Tip: Tilt your head and use a questioning facial expression when using this sign.

---

wind

Swing the 5 hands from side to side.

Memory aid: Show the wind blowing.

Tip: Blow air out of your mouth while signing.

window

Rest the little finger of the right Open B hand on the index finger of the left hand, and then raise the right hand a few inches and bring it back down.

Memory aid: Show a window opening and closing.

Tip: If your windows open from side to side, you can sign *window* with B hands by moving one hand to the side and back again. This form of the sign also can be used for *sliding door.* The meaning will depend on the context of your sentence.

winter

Shake the W hands in very small motions toward each other several times.

Memory aid: The W hands represent *winter,* and they are shivering from the cold.

wolf

Put the fingertips of the right Bent 5 hand around the nose. Then pull the hand away from the face while changing it into a Flat O hand.

Memory aid: Show the long nose of a wolf.

woman

Touch the chin with the thumb of the right A hand, bring the hand down to the chest while changing to a 5 hand, and end with the thumb on the chest.

Memory aid: The lower part of the cheek and chin are the female areas of the face, and the chest position indicates the idea of sophistication; thus, a *woman* is a sophisticated *girl*.

---

wonderful, great, super, terrific

Push both 5 hands out several times.

Tip: Be sure to have a happy facial expression. The pushing motion of the sign is not strong but more subtle.

---

work, job

Tap the right S hand against the side of the left S hand a couple of times.

Tip: This sign can be used as a noun or as a verb.

worm

Bend and straighten the right index finger as it slides down the left palm.

Memory aid: Picture a worm inching its way across the hand.

yellow

Twist the right Y hand from side to side several times.

yes

Bend the wrist of the right S hand up and down.

Memory aid: You nod your head when saying yes.

yesterday

Touch the corner of the mouth with the thumb of the right A hand, then move it back and touch the cheek.

Memory aid: Move backward in time.

Tip: The Y hand may be used in place of the A hand. The Y represents the initial letter of *yesterday.*

---

yogurt

Scoop the little finger of the right Y hand out of the left palm several times.

Memory aid: Think of scooping yogurt out of a bowl.

---

zebra (1)

Place the thumb of the right H hand on the right temple and bend the extended fingers down. Then move the right 4 hand across the chest.

Memory aid: A zebra is a horse with stripes.

zebra (2)

Place the fingertips of the right 4 hand on the left side of the chest and the fingertips of the left 4 hand on the right side of the chest; move the hands across the chest.

Memory aid: The stripes of the zebra.

zipper

Place both X hands, with the thumbs tucked inside the index fingers, at the waist. Then raise the right hand straight up.

Memory aid: Mimic zipping up a jacket.

O

P

T

Y

Z